Dear Rabbi David,

May the impact of your life be as great as a lion's roar.

A LION'S ROAR

Fear, Courage and Whispers of Change

Rosenblatt

SONIA ROSENBLATT

ISBN: 978-1-5272-2353-0

First published in 2018

To my precious and gentle Bandit.
Your light lives within me.

To all animals everywhere who have suffered
and are suffering at the hands of mankind.

Author's Note

To write this book, I relied upon my personal journal, researched facts when I could, consulted with several of the people who appear in this book, and called upon my own memory of these events and this time of my life. I have changed the names of most but not all of the individuals in my book, and in some cases I have also modified details in order to preserve anonymity. There are no composite characters in this book. I omitted people and events, only when the omission had no impact on either the authenticity or the substance of the story. Some events have been compressed and some dialogue has been recreated.

The views expressed in this book are mine only, and do not represent those of any organisation or individual contained in this book.

Acknowledgements

A heartfelt thank you to Richard McMunn and Jordan Cooke at the Book Publishing Academy for your encouragement and helpful feedback, and for transforming my manuscript into this book. Thank you Jordan for your endless patience and gentle guidance. Thank you both for believing in me.

I am deeply thankful to Susan Ryan whose insightful edits and razor-sharp eye for detail helped me transform my ramblings into a crafted piece of prose.

A big thank you goes to all the dedicated staff at African Conservation Experience who bring dreams to life for people like myself.

Thank you to the staff at Moholoholo Wildlife Rehabilitation Centre, Tuli Wilderness, Hanchi Horseback Conservation and Phinda Private Game Reserve—modern day heroes in the fight to protect our natural environment.

Finally, I would like to express my deepest love and gratitude to my mother and father whose love and unwavering support carried me through this journey.

The walls in my apartment are blue. In the light of day, they are a shade somewhere between sea and sky. At night, as I lie awake into the early hours, these walls become a deep ocean blue that closes in around me. I stare into the blue. It stares back. Leaning back, my eyes follow the line upward to where two walls meet, the cheap metal Ikea chair squeaking with my every move. At the top of the wall, a small white line extends all the way around, almost disappearing into the mottled ceiling of jutted stucco. The silence is deafening.

Framed by darkness, the white glare of my laptop screen blurs before my eyes. The cursor hovers over yet another job application, frozen in place, blinking urgently. I place my head in my hands and sigh. Crying does not get anyone anywhere, ever.

Alone with nothing but time and my thoughts, my mind roams to those who have hurt me, not only in the past year, but also in the past three decades. My primary school days at a small Jewish school in Dublin were nurturing, growing up in the bubble of a tight-knit community, surrounded by friends known since birth. Those same friends joined the same youth groups, and we all shared similar interests. However, I always knew that at the age of twelve, I would not be attending the Jewish secondary school alongside my friends. Instead, I would go to a Protestant secondary school, the same one my father had attended. In my parents' eyes, this would provide me with a more rounded education that would better prepare me for life's challenges.

On my first day at that school, I learned two things. The first was that I did not fit in. The second was that people were mean. As a shy, awkward, lanky teenager with a mouthful of braces, I stood in the courtyard outside the portacabin classroom door with my new classmates, waiting for the teacher to arrive. They all seemed to know each other having moved collectively from a couple of local primary schools. They snickered and pointed at me, whispering. I had contravened the strict uniform rules that extended to shoe colour, not intentionally, but because my mother was unable to find a pair of black or brown shoes that fit me. We settled on grey. Nine hundred pupils attended the school—more people than I had ever seen in one place before. There were only a dozen Jewish pupils, three of whom were in my class.

Ripped from the comfort of the only world I knew, I floundered in the one that followed. Having known all my friends from early childhood, I had never really needed to learn to socialise with new people. For a whole year, barely anyone spoke to me. I sat alone in class and at lunch or, if they let me, I could share a table with my classmates. Although I made friends as the years progressed, the bullying and teasing about my prominent Jewish features were a part of my everyday life. I was ugly, different. No one came to my birthday party. For ten years, these experiences lingered quietly beneath the surface of my conscious thoughts, manifesting themselves as a recurring nightmare of never having permission to leave school.

In my early twenties, in the 1990s, the Dublin Jewish community dwindled. I too moved to London in the wave of emigration made by my peers seeking a larger Jewish community elsewhere, acquiring a language degree in French and Spanish, and joining the working world. After six years in London, I was fatigued from the daily grind, a grey life under grey skies, a persistent cough constantly exacerbated by dangerous levels of toxic pollution, and weakened from bouts of anxiety that would suddenly grip me while waiting below ground for the next tube. Sometimes, a kind person would sit on the bench beside me until the panic subsided, but more often than not, I suffered alone in silence as the throngs of people ebbed and flowed along the platform, unaware of my torment. I did not know then that these forces that came out of nowhere had a name, nor that I could have sought advice.

Feeling anonymous and swallowed up by a large city without the support I craved, I dreamed of a simpler life, one of space and clean air, one of friends and joyous celebrations. Although my brother and extended family were also in London, they were consumed with their own lives. My parents were still living in Dublin. There was no reason for me to stay in London.

By now, I was ready for change. Daughters of distant friends of my parents had recently moved to Canada, quickly settling, finding jobs, a husband and a supportive network. Ostensibly, they were happy there. I started to mull the idea over, asking work colleagues, friends and people I met randomly about what they knew of this land of maple leaves, beavers, ice hockey, poutine, boreal forests, snow-capped mountains and prairies. All responses were positive. Some had been there on holiday, but most had heard good things second-hand. Over the course of a year and a half, I applied for permanent residency, making two one-week trips to Toronto during that time.

At the age of twenty-seven, I moved to Toronto with two suitcases. I did not own much. Although it was daunting to build a life across the ocean, I was determined that this new chapter would bring what all my years in London had lacked. I had no job, a month of accommodation in place, and I only knew a handful of people. My parents flew out with me, staying for a month. Then I was on my own. The day they left, I walked around my new neighbourhood under warm April skies, trying to make my unfamiliar surroundings familiar, pushing down the disquiet at feeling very alone.

Over the decade in Toronto, I experienced both the best days of my life and days that felt unsurmountable. My very first job, secured within six weeks of my arrival, was at a foreign exchange company where my new colleagues saw fit to circulate a drawing, a caricature of sorts, exaggerating my Jewish features. They laughed as they denied that it was of anyone in particular. This experience prompted me to put an end to three decades of relentless teasing with rhinoplasty. It was a thirtieth birthday gift to myself—a gift of sanity. Of course, they found other ways to torment me. They threw balls of paper at the spiral pattern on my jumper. Target practice, they called it. They ignored me and never invited me for lunch. My invitations to join me for lunch were met with forgettable excuses.

Fresh off the boat in a country I hardly knew, I felt powerless to complain. However, as with all forms of incremental harassment, I reached a tipping point. Even though I exceeded targets, and performed far better than my predecessor, after six months, the thought of another day there was unbearable. I resigned. So deeply affected by this experience, seven years later, when it came to writing a paper for my Ethics in Business course as part of my graduate degree, previously unshed tears flowed freely as I analysed what had happened to me through the psychology of group behaviour.

Other jobs followed, driven mostly by the need to pay bills. Almost none of them aligned with my values. Over the years, no matter how hard I tried to conceal my anxiety, my employers sniffed out the scent of my sensitivity. In their eyes, it was a character flaw, a sign of inexcusable weakness. Each time they knocked me down, I dusted myself off and bounced back—never stronger, but a little wiser—only to be knocked down again.

Repeatedly, I found myself in toxic work environments, expected perhaps in the financial and banking sectors. The frequent berating, and the sustained and prolonged periods of job insecurity often threatened my mental wellness, pushing me beyond anxiety, and into the darkness of depression. The last two contracts were by far the worst, surprising given that these fields had better reputations. At an environmental consulting department, at a university in a town nearby, my female boss would demand that her unrealistic expectations be met or be subject to her unrelenting and scorching rebukes, which were often delivered in front of my colleagues or over the phone on a Friday evening when I worked from home.

Immediately following this position, at a small not-for-profit consulting firm, working under yet another woman with an A-type personality, when handed a pile of documents, I was not allowed to ask questions until she reached the end of a long list of instructions, nor was I allowed to look at pages other than the one my boss was discussing. Her questions demanded snappy immediate answers or be subjected to her derision. Her controlling and exacting measures even extended to the final day of my contract. Collecting my belongings, still needing to hand back the office key, I put on my coat, slung my bag over my shoulder, and walked hesitantly into her office. I never knew what mood would greet me, her celiac disease made her unpredictable. Snatching the key from my hands, she held it up in the air to examine it, and then pressed her key against mine to verify that the grooves matched, to prove that the key was in fact hers. Speechless, I stood in front of her desk, having never been treated with such disdain and mistrust.

Despite challenges in the workplace, I considered myself lucky to be in a position to buy a nice apartment in Midtown Toronto. A nifty Toyota Echo gave me independence, and often relieved me of trudging through feet of snow, and bracing myself in sub-zero temperatures. I made friends too, making it my business to introduce each one to another. My Jewish friends marvelled at how they all knew each other because of me, though they never introduced me to their outer circles. Having kept the same group of friends from school, it did not occur to them. They took for granted that which I never could.

Now these friends have all but gone—each one following the same predictable pattern: moving from singledom to the smug world of coupledom, promising to meet, vowing to introduce me to their new circle. Promises were broken, plans invariably and perpetually postponed, and always at the last minute. Inevitably, the calls stopped coming completely. I no longer fitted into their lives. Their choice of husband perplexed me. Shuddering at the thought of being married to any one of them, I felt a sense of courage that I had not succumbed to societal pressures, nor to the pitiful pool of men from which they had chosen.

Boyfriends too have come and gone, each one following a similar pattern of falling in love with me, or breaking my heart. I grew tired of meeting men who slurped, who cut their food with the side of a fork, whose only interest was ice hockey, and whose lazy dress sense resembled every other man I would meet—beige shorts, a faded t-shirt, and Birkenstock sandals. In an effort to make my heart theirs, they ditched these habits. One almost succeeded, becoming unrecognisable in clothes that fit, and were of this century. Once suited, booted, coiffed and considerably slimmer, he married another, reverting almost immediately to his old ways. However, one man filled my life on and off for five years. In the end, he decided I was no longer a convenient option.

Unemployed three times in the past eighteen months, and now six months since my last job, I shuffle from room to room in my Toronto apartment of blue walls and white stucco ceilings. My body hunches over from the weight of the entire world sitting on my shoulders. Constantly tired, I get up late every day, busying myself with arranging and reorganising my space, clinging to the faint hope that the distraction will calm the hurricane of questions swirling incessantly in my brain. *How did my life derail so far off the course I set myself? How will I get myself back on track? What should I do with my life? Should I move elsewhere? Why am I alone and unemployed yet again? What's wrong with me?* The why and how go endlessly on. No matter how many times I ask, the answers never come.

After a few hours of menial tasks, I resign myself to job hunting. By early afternoon, I am back in bed in a foetal position. It is not due to an under-commitment to goals, but an over-commitment to those failing badly that leaves me overwhelmed. The phone rings. I ignore it. I know it is my mother. My friends no longer call and my extended family living three thousand miles away have long since forgotten me. Although my mother has the best of intentions, her insistence to know what my next steps will be is not something I can deal with today. Tuning out the ringing until it stops, I let her leave yet another message.

I stare blankly at my vision board on the wall, a small corkboard with pictures cut out of magazines over the years. Pinned to the cork are places I dream of going, and words and images that resonate with my being. A drawing of a polar bear sits atop an ice floe. There is a Toyota Prius and a simple sketch of a dog and cat. The words "protection" and "peace" sit beside a picture of people trekking through a tropical rainforest. A tree house perched high above the forest floor sits next to a picture of a stunning black and white ball gown with a purple sash, by a Spanish designer who shares my first name.

I know vision boards work. Just three years earlier, I spent two weeks in the rainforests of Costa Rica. It was a requirement of my graduate degree research in environmental sustainability. Only on my return did I realise that the images on my vision board cut out five years earlier had manifested into reality, completely unplanned, occurring in a way I could never have imagined. My eyes fall on the other pictures pinned there, but nothing stirs me. The dreams they once promised seem to have vanished. I stare at them vacantly until unshed tears blur my vision, and the images blend into nothing.

My only source of comfort is my fourteen-year-old black and white cat, adopted earlier in the year when I was still grief-stricken at the death of my cat Nala who graced my life for nine years. It was not my intention to adopt another cat, not for a good while anyway. However, in December, after meeting a man whose pregnant Asian girlfriend was curiously suddenly allergic to his two fourteen-year-old cats he adopted as kittens, I agreed to take one of them, sparing him from a tirade of disgust and disbelief that he would pander to her whim of having his beloved cats rehomed. I adopted Bandit, so called because of her distinctive markings—black patches over the eyes, separated by a band of white sloping down her nose to a triangle of black at the tip—it was love at first sight.

Bandit follows me everywhere, often jumping up onto my round glass table to sit on the very document that needs my attention. She curls up on the bed beside me, purring so loudly that it sometimes renders sleep impossible. So utterly content, she often lays on her back soaking up the beams of sunshine captured by the ceiling-to-floor windows.

Although she hardly ever meows, instinctively I know when she is hungry or wants to go out on the balcony. I know when she wants attention and when she wants to be alone. She listens to me, blinking slowly. I know she understands me, but most of all, I know that she knows that I love her. That is of utmost importance to me. We have precious moments where I feel a tingling of my soul—an innate knowing that my bond with her is beyond my logical understanding. I envy Bandit sometimes; her uncomplicated life is filled with simple pleasures—catnip, beams of sunshine, and feathers slithering across the hardwood floor. Uncomplaining, she just *is*, always in the moment. My life would be utterly pointless without her. She is my only reason to get up in the morning.

No one hires now in the summer months, nor in the run-up to the end of the year. Questions of why I have been out of work for so many months are becoming increasingly difficult to answer. Portraying an air of confidence and positivity proves more challenging with every passing day. My forced enthusiasm and desperate attempts to hide my fear of endless unemployment seem to be evident to everyone except me.

However, in September, an invitation to interview for a very well-paid job in the field of environmental sustainability gives me renewed hope. Perhaps my luck is about to change. I prepare night and day, meeting experts beforehand in the hope that inside industry knowledge will somehow give me the edge. I am pleased with my efforts since these days just leaving the house requires great will and determination. Despite my preparations, the interview is a train wreck. Unable to answer a simple question at the start, my nerves unhinge me. My brain struggles to provide the right answers while my body tells me to terminate the interview early and run for the door. Instead, I steel myself and stay until the end, leaving dignified and poised but in no doubt that all chances of getting that job lay tattered on the floor.

I spend the next few days painfully analysing every detail of how I managed to let this opportunity slip through my fingers. I did everything right but also everything wrong. I feel broken and overwrought, incapable of presenting basic ideas that I spent two years studying. Endless days of loneliness, emptiness, and a dwindling bank account lay bleakly in front of me. The thought alone is frightening, and I know the reality will be far worse.

Loathing my constant wallowing in self-pity, I decide that if change is not going to come to me, then I am going to have to *make* change. I need to take action, to DO something—ANYTHING—other than sit in my apartment day and night doing the same thing repeatedly and expecting the same outcome. I feel as if I am slowly descending into madness.

My need to escape, from people and my life in general, is all-consuming. Never allowing my practical side to be suspended, I decide that my escape must include the acquisition of a useful skill. I begin to wonder if perhaps improving my French will help me land a highly coveted bilingual position.

With the decision made that this is my best course of action, I search for a three-month intensive language course for adults, one that can build upon my latent but not forgotten linguistic ability that secured me a job fifteen years earlier. Preferring the sound of Metropolitan French to that spoken by Canadians, the sparsely populated French territories of St. Pierre and Michelon, located twelve miles south of the Canadian island of Newfoundland, pique my interest.

With diminishing funds, there is no choice but to sell my apartment—my home for the past ten years. I push all sentiment down and make the call to a local estate agent. Within days, my apartment is on the market and staged for viewing. It is neutral, impersonal and completely void of the occupant's essence. Two weeks later, with a shaking hand and a thumping heart, I sign the bottom line. I have two months to hand over the keys.

I decide that most of my belongings will go into storage and I will either sell or donate the rest. The garage sale, organised the day after Nala passed, left me with far fewer items to sort. Some days I pack with defiance, thumbing my nose at all who have sought to push me down and all those who have abandoned me. Set to leave behind ten years of a life that I have built for myself, who here will care?

Other days I pack with a heavy heart and a crushing sense of sadness. Such needless upheaval. If only things were different. Using one of the many boxes as leverage, I wearily push myself up off my bedroom floor and remove the vision board from the wall. With a gentle pull, each picture is freed from the spike of a multi-coloured thumbtack. I unpin the tiny picture of a girl. I remember the day she caught my eye in a conservation magazine; the picture stopped me in my tracks. Dressed in a beige t-shirt and trousers, her long hair is pulled back in a ponytail, a cheetah lays on the ground in front of her. The surrounding landscape, and the white safari Jeep, suggests she is in Africa. Slumped back down on the floor, I tell myself that if I close my eyes tightly and wish hard enough, I will BE that girl. When I open my eyes, I am still crumpled on the floor. With a sinking heart, I toss her into a box, confining her and other such dreams to darkness as I close the lid.

My mind is now set on studying in a tiny, remote village, completely cut off from the rest of society. I busy myself with the application forms, but I do not feel quite as elated or excited as I had hoped. While the decision to study French in a faraway place in the depths of winter feeds my need for considered solitude, I am still hesitant to make it concrete. This procrastination makes me wonder if I have really made the right decision. Vacillating between certainty and hesitation, I finally delay submitting payment. Without a clear course of action, I lapse into another bout of mindless and incapacitating numbness. During this time, an email catches my eye, almost lost among the dozens of generic job application rejection letters. It is an invitation to join a university acquaintance at the *Go Global Expo*, a fair promoting volunteer programmes around the world. On the day of the expo, my friend calls to say she cannot attend but urges me to go anyway.

The expo conference room heaves with people. Rows of stands with glossy brochures and backdrops vie for volunteers. I dismiss humanitarian projects. While building houses and teaching children in poor countries are crucial services, they do not interest me. I take brochures from all stands promoting conservation projects. At the *African Conservation Experience* stand, people clamber for information. Although I am desperate to talk to the representative, I do not have the energy to push myself to the front of the crowd nor the patience to wait and be jostled in the process. Instead, I grab a brochure and add it to the growing pile stuffed in the conference bag weighing heavily on my arm. The crowd pushes again, and I begin to feel claustrophobic. It is hot, airless and loud, and I suddenly need to get out. With my panic levels rising, my eyes frantically search for an exit sign. When I finally make my way out, the quiet and coolness of the lobby calms me. I glance at the escalator leading towards the exit but find myself drawn to a small room down the corridor.

Representatives from a handful of companies tend to a few curious attendees. To my surprise, there is another *African Conservation Experience* booth with a representative waiting for visitors. Weary, I sit down on a chair and exchange pleasantries. Large picture albums on the table quickly capture my attention. Elephants, cheetahs, rhinos, lions, leopards, whales, dolphins, and animals I have never even seen before, beckon me to stay awhile. Blazing red sunsets in exotic places, and magnificent images of animal relocation, rehabilitation and cohabitation, gently flutter the corners of my soul.

A thousand questions come to mind as I examine each picture with rapture and delight, but my practical side is whispering with exceptionally good reasons why I would be better served spending the next three months acquiring a skill that would improve my employability. My heart, on the other hand, begs my soul to listen. Ms. Practical wins. A practical solution to finding a stable job is what I should be concentrating on, not spending my time and money on a childish dream at such a critical time of my life. I interrupt the representative mid-sentence, close the albums, and stand up rather abruptly, causing the chair to fall over. I thank the woman for her time, but apologise for wasting it. I leave despondent, confused, and perturbed. My down-filled The North Face winter coat and heavy boots seem all the more burdensome as I drag myself home.

For the next few days, the fogginess and numbness I feel make even the smallest task impossible. I stay in my pyjamas all day slouched in front of the TV, flicking mindlessly through the channels. Instead of cooking, I order my favourite Indian dishes from the local takeaway, sending me into an addictive food coma. I leave my dirty dishes in the living room overnight. My laundry piles up. I do not even make my bed. Reaching a decision as to what I will do once I hand over the apartment keys feels insurmountable. Frightened I am falling into a one-way pit of despair, I leave Bandit with my neighbour and fly to Dublin to stay with my parents for one week.

I sleep soundly and without nightmares for the first time in weeks, waking up to the birds singing, to breakfast in bed and constant loving attention. I feel my spirits lifting and the haziness that usually plagues my every waking hour is surprisingly absent. It feels good to reconnect with old friends. They all encourage me to follow my heart.

Curled up beside the gas fire with a cup of hot chocolate, I look at the array of brochures laid out on the floor. Each image sends my mind down different pathways, igniting different sensations in my body. However, Ms. Practical is still present. My mother joins me on the white leather couch, followed by a waft of homemade chicken soup emanating from the kitchen. "Follow your passion," she says. I call *African Conservation Experience.*

For as long as I can remember, I have felt a special connection with animals. At five years old, I stood in front of the television and screamed. A cat trapped on the upper floors in the film *Towering Inferno* was too much for me to bear. My ear-splitting cries stopped only when the cat was safely outside. I desperately wanted to meet Mowgli, believing that such a boy existed. I once found a cat injured on the roadside and rushed it to the vet. Even though I had only known it for half an hour, I sobbed after it passed away. During my gap year in Mexico, I adopted two flea-ridden homeless cats. We had one cat at home, although I always wanted more. When I am out, I scan the streets for dogs without owners, often following seemingly stray dogs only to find their owners a little way behind. I had a knack too of coaxing frightened cats at animal shelters, some impossible to be handled even by staff, to sit calmly on my lap.

Now, I can barely believe my life is taking me to Africa. My childhood consisted of regular doses of Attenborough-narrated nature programmes. While my father revelled in the chase between predator and prey, my mother refused to watch. Caught between those opposing perspectives, I watched transfixed but in an impossible dilemma. Should I root for the young zebra foal running for his life on wobbly legs or for the lion cubs who would starve if their mother returned unsuccessful yet again? My heart thumped wildly, and no matter what the outcome I always felt sad. Although, however seemingly cruel the circle of life may be, it is man who has created an imbalance between winners and losers.

Our planet is dying at the hands of our greed and avarice; the delicate equilibrium of our ecosystem shunted towards a place beyond recognition. When did we forget that we have borrowed the earth from our children and seven generations beyond? We have decimated entire species and have perilously endangered others in a relentless pursuit of riches and power. I cannot bear any form of animal suffering or abuse, or any situation where an animal cannot engage in its natural behaviour and live out its life free of pain and fear. Trophy hunting, animal trafficking, animal testing, factory farming, zoos and circuses are only some of the seemingly never-ending ways that humans, albeit mainly men, torture and inflict indescribable suffering on innocent animals. These crimes are beyond my comprehension.

After lengthy discussions with *African Conservation Experience*, I decide against marine conservation projects because my one and only experience with diving made me feel claustrophobic. I rule out game capture and relocation projects, knowing that this would likely be far too stressful for me. I finally settle on three projects, two in South Africa and one in Botswana. For the first four weeks, I choose Moholoholo Wildlife Rehabilitation Centre, a haven for abandoned, injured and poisoned wildlife. For the following four weeks, I pick the Phinda Private Game Reserve to work alongside a conservation research team conducting big cat, rhino and elephant monitoring. Then it will be Tuli Wilderness in Botswana for the final four weeks, including a one-week intensive Game Ranger course to learn animal tracking and the use of a firearm. Due to the sheer remoteness of this particular project and the absence of electricity, I decide to go there last, knowing that I will need the previous two months to work up to such an extreme environment.

My choices now made, I say goodbye to my parents in Dublin and fly back to Toronto to wind down the life I know. With a clear goal and deadline set, and an innate ability to organise logistics, I have no problem arranging the remaining myriad of tasks. I continue to sort my belongings into four distinct groups—sell, keep, donate, bin—choosing the fourth option only if absolutely necessary because I know that these items will remain in a landfill for many decades to come. It only takes me a split second to decide if I would be happy to see an item again. If so, it goes in the keep pile. I take pictures of everything I want to sell and post them on classified ad sites. The calls and visits from buyers are a welcome reprieve from the solitude. I look at the wish lists of my favourite charities, gather what I can and hand-deliver the items.

I consider what to do with my array of broken, old and tarnished costume jewellery hanging neatly on a wall hanger in my walk-in wardrobe. I google "donate costume jewellery". Just a few hours later, I hand over my jewellery to a therapist running creative workshops for abused women. Her gratitude at unexpectedly receiving much-needed supplies and my pleasure of finding a "home" for my unwanted items, make our twenty-minute exchange in the lobby of my apartment building one of the most fulfilling I have had in months. I cancel my utilities, fix the broken wing mirror before posting my car online and call a few companies to find the best quote for temporary storage. A friend offers to store my bed, which allows me to rent a smaller storage unit. I take advantage of still having the car to go back and forth to the packing shop to buy more boxes and supplies.

A friend I have known for five years agrees to come to my apartment for a couple of hours on the day I have arranged viewings of my remaining furniture. I would prefer not be alone since I do not know who will come to the door. By the way she constantly glances at her watch and shifts restlessly on my Ikea Ektorp two-seater couch, I can tell she would rather be elsewhere. I will have two days left in Toronto after I hand over my keys, arranged purposely to tidy up last-minute loose ends and to make several trips back and forth to the apartment to meet with the estate agent. Without my car on those last few days, staying nearby would afford me enormous convenience, not least to avoid trekking back and forth on public transport in frigid temperatures. I ask my friend if I could possibly stay with her for two nights since her flat is only a few minutes' walk from mine.

Fumbling in her oversized handbag, she busies herself with searching for something that suddenly has great importance. While rummaging, I continue to explain just how grateful I would be. She puts her bag down on the floor and leans forward, folding her arms on her long black skirt. "I'm afraid that's not possible," she says. "My husband won't like you to be around while I am at work." Married only weeks earlier to an Australian, who was now job hunting from their flat, I understand that he would not want to be disturbed during the day, especially while adjusting to married life far from his family and friends down under. Even though I relay that I only need a bed for two nights, still she refuses. I recoil internally, retreating behind my wall of protection built all those years ago. My cheek winces. Although I do not yet fully comprehend the full extent of the insult she has laid upon me, I tell her I completely understand. Our eyes meet. Our goodbye is awkward.

Only one problem truly weighs heavy on my mind. I plan to be abroad for at least three months and I do not know if I will return permanently to Canada. What to do with Bandit is a constant source of anguish. The only thing I know for sure is that I will come back for her once the trip is over. There is no question about that. To me, this is a temporary arrangement, an extended holiday. I start with everyone I know, but no one is interested in temporarily fostering her. The weeks pass quickly and my move-out deadline for the middle of December is looming. Resolute that I will not leave the country unless I have found a suitable home for her, I decide that I will even delay my trip if I have not found a solution. On this, I will not budge.

I had considered leaving Bandit with my parents, but the long flight, cost and logistics involved seemed prohibitive for such a short time. Completely out of options, I finally resort to posting a flyer with Bandit's picture in my local supermarket. Miraculously, I get two responses. Bandit and I meet both Laura and Alice. I decide that Alice is my first choice. Laura will be a backup if anything should go wrong. My gut feeling and absence of warning bells tell me that both women are trustworthy and there is no need to worry. This comforts me.

In the days before handing over the keys, my apartment looks and feels soulless. I will for these last few days to be over. Boxes line the length of one wall. I have spent the past week eating from one plate and one set of cutlery because everything is packed, and I cannot bring myself to eat yet another restaurant meal alone. The sparse ill-placed pot lights provide only the bare minimum of light. The TV is bubble wrapped and with nothing left to do, I sit on a box in half darkness, asking Bandit to forgive me for our temporary separation.

The day that I must drive Bandit to Alice's house finally arrives. I steel myself. This is one of the hardest decisions I have ever had to make. Although not quite as bad as the decision to put Nala to sleep, the pain is equally acute. Alice answers the door, and I immediately tell her not to talk to me because tears are coming and I know if they start, I will fall apart completely. Bandit is curious and exploratory when I let her out of her carrier, taking in her new home without any sign of distress. I wonder why I need to worry about her. As I wish her goodbye, she does not look up or seem to care. I am both hurt and relieved. In order to put an end to my agony, I leave hastily, barely reconciling parting with my greatest treasure.

A lovely couple promises to take care of my car as I had done. Already second hand, I had only clocked up thirty-five thousand kilometres over seven years. As they drive off, I remind myself that it is only an inanimate object and there is no reason to be upset. Pushing all sentiment aside, I go back upstairs to tackle the logistics of transporting my belongings to the self-storage unit.

Most of my requests for help with loading my boxes into a U-Haul van are ignored. However, one friend does help me out, a French girl also planning to move overseas. We spend a gruelling ten hours loading and unloading the van, and then arranging my belongings into a 5x5ft storage unit. Mercifully, the husband of a university friend drives the van to the storage facility over twenty kilometres away, too terrified myself to drive such a large vehicle with no back windows.

Old friends of my parents invite me to stay the two nights before I leave Toronto, their kindness extended to me once again in my hour of need. They had been so kind to me especially in my first few months in Canada, their reassuring words, invites for dinner and marvels at my courage at moving country alone made me feel invincible, albeit fleetingly.

The events in my final few weeks leave me drained and emotionally spent. In the airport departure lounge, I check my phone for last-minute goodbyes but there are none. I board the plane to Dublin bereft of spirit but in no doubt at all that I have made the right decision.

Camping shops in Dublin's Northside are my first port of call. The narrow streets are not designed for the number of cars now grinding to another standstill. The grimy footpaths and old grey buildings are comforting in their familiarity rather than a source of irritation of their neglect. I know these streets well; my parents' business is not far from here. With a suggested packing list in hand, I gather the items I need, sauntering from one shop to the next. I already have a side-opening backpack from several camping trips to Algonquin Park, a four-hour drive from Toronto, with my on-then-off-again ex-boyfriend. I am sure that not having to take out the items at the top to get at the items at the bottom will be a feature I will come to appreciate. Mesmerised by the array of binoculars on offer, I finally choose a mid-range Bushnell 8x21. I buy a headlamp with three settings, a mosquito net encased in a bright orange bag, and a foldable waterproof jacket and trousers—one navy, the other black since matching colours were not available in my size. Both are too big for me anyway. I also buy a pair of lightweight but sturdy boots.

As the sales assistant runs through the unique features of each item at my request, I chuckle to myself and think of my on-then-off-again ex-boyfriend. I would be unrecognisable to him now. I would gently tease him when he spent hours poring over internet descriptions of camping equipment and clothing. He had dreams of owning a shop selling outdoor gear in British Columbia. He could reel off the unique features of countless items of the most well-known brands. Until he took me camping, I had no appreciation for the smallest of details that would often provide the greatest of comfort—nor had I an appreciation for the different types of materials that could either lighten or burden the load. If nothing else, he gave me the gift of this appreciation.

Refusing to over pack, I pack carefully. Everything has a practical purpose; except for one item of vanity that I have allowed myself—a small hair straightener to tame my unruly curly hair. I pack a few books including one on African wildlife and a Southern Africa travel guide. It was never part of the plan to bring my phone, deciding that I will rent a basic non-smartphone at the airport in Johannesburg for emergencies only. Wishing to be free of anything that links me to the outside world, I will not bring my laptop or even my prized but far too cumbersome SLR. I settle for a simple point-and-click camera.

The day before my departure for an overnight stay with my brother in London, I check the contents of my backpack yet again, opened flat on my double bed. Having already spent hours deciding which compartment would be best suited for each item for the greatest ease of access, my clothes are rolled carefully to maximise space and minimise creasing, then laid neatly side-by-side, similar colours of grey, black, white, brown and green grouped together. My boots and other shoes fit nicely inside the large outside pocket. Internal mesh pockets of different sizes are home to smaller items. A quick drying towel sits beside my waterproofs. Finally satisfied, I pull up the zippers, the purring of the teeth as they embrace in perfect alignment adding to my rising anticipation. I place my backpack beside the front door, the black behemoth standing guard until I rise the next morning.

Crippling anxiety grips me on the morning of my flight from London, in sharp contrast to when I said goodbye to my parents and boarded the flight from Dublin just the day before. I was composed and excited with only a tinge of trepidation as to what the next twelve weeks would bring. The previous twenty-four hours were free of any strong unhinging emotion and I was rather pleased with myself that I felt so calm. Now, I clutch the side of the bed and focus on the beige tufty carpet in an effort to calm a full-blown panic attack. The thought of leaving the safety of this small guest room and entering into the unknown is terrifying. My mind churns through all the reasons why I cannot leave. *What if I really don't love animals that much after all? Bandit will miss me too much and I should really*

go back for her as soon as possible. Maybe I just chose the wrong projects? And there's that party I want to attend. I even have thoughts that my life was not so bad—that I need to go back to Toronto and make it work. Big reasons and tiny reasons, real reasons and silly reasons, all equally weighted and make perfect sense in my mind, though I know they would quickly fall apart if I said them aloud.

The taxi pulls up outside. My brother and sister-in-law call to me from downstairs, their urgency only exacerbating the rising nausea. My hands grip the sheets as I take deep breaths and ride the wave of blindsiding panic. The only way to get myself downstairs is to trick my brain. I tell myself I just need to make it a few steps to the bathroom. With all the energy I can muster, I push myself off the bed, hold onto the doorframe, and propel myself over the landing and into the bathroom. Ice-cold water gives me momentary reprieve, but I am shocked when I see my reflection in the mirror. Pallid, waxen and with a fresh outbreak of acne, I barely recognise myself. In a haze, I make it down the stairs, holding onto the bannister as my feet thud on every step. Outside in the crisp January air, I hug my six-year-old niece, then turn to my one-year-old niece sleeping in my brother's arms and kiss her softly on the forehead. Hastily, I hug my brother and his wife as both wish me well. I nod fervently willing the goodbyes to be over before I change my mind.

Travel sickness pills relieve me from the monotony and cramped conditions of travelling economy class. I sleep deeply for more than half of the eleven-hour journey, providing reprieve from my mind straining to pinpoint the exact cause of my anxiety. After all, I am going on an adventure of my choosing based on my deepest passions. However, the root cause of anxiety is often hard to isolate.

Martin, a burly *African Conservation Experience* representative, meets me at Johannesburg airport and introduces me to the other volunteers. We are a small bunch from around the globe. Straightaway, I feel as if I am part of a special group and I immediately warm to my new companions. Maybe it is his strong South African accent or his enthusiastic and reassuring manner, but the anxiety that has been gripping me for the past twenty-four hours is finally easing.

A large black SUV whisks us away, travelling northeast for seven hours. We ride in animated chatter, eager to know why each of us has chosen a sharp departure from our normal life. There are long periods of silence too. Lulled by the steady motion of the van as it speeds along the motorway and tired from the long flight, we slip into an easy silence, each of us absorbed in our own thoughts.

We arrive late evening at the *Moholoholo Wildlife Rehabilitation Centre*. Having left such cold temperatures, I immediately notice the warm night air as I get out of the vehicle. I am enveloped by the drone of cicadas pulsing through the air, the chirping of crickets and the whooping of hyena. Lisa welcomes us to the girls' volunteer accommodation with a broad smile. She is homely, her face slightly weather-beaten and dressed in the Moholoholo (The Great One) staff uniform of an ankle-length cream skirt and greyish shirt. Strict modesty rules require that staff and volunteers cover their knees and shoulders. Moths flutter around the naked light bulbs, casting dancing shadows on the ochre walls of the single storey concrete building. The younger volunteers will share a dorm for ten. For once, I am pleased that my age is affording me an advantage. Lisa shows me to my bedroom. It is rustic with a simple wardrobe, a wooden table and chair and ensuite bathroom. Two single beds, each with a wooden nightstand and lamp lay under the window. The concrete floor is shiny and meticulously clean. A large camera bag and clothes folded neatly on the other bed belong to Susan, my roommate who arrived a few days earlier. A black scrapbook open to the middle reveals a small pencil sketch of an owl at the top left corner of the brown page. I put my backpack flat on the floor beside my bed. The first item I reach for is the bright orange pouch. I remove my shoes and stand on the bed, hoping that I am tall enough to affix the mosquito net to the hooks on the ceiling. I look around. I am satisfied that this will be my home for the next four weeks.

Although each day brings a different delight, there is a similar daily routine. My alarm clock wakes me at 6 a.m. and I whisper to Susan that I will see her at the clinic. Not being a morning person, I prefer not to engage in chat this early. I slip into light-grey trousers and a baggy beige t-shirt with a Moholoholo logo. Stepping outside into the morning air, allowing the warmth of the sun to fall gently on my face, I shake my boots to cast out any insects that may have been using them as a home overnight. My five-minute walk to work this morning will be void of pneumatic drills, circular saws, snow blowers, car engines, beeping, ringing, and the general grating din of city life. Instead, I walk to the tune of beautiful birdsong, accompanied by a cacophony of wildlife.

Opposite my bedroom door, spotted hyenas, Shade, Shadow and baby Luma, sleep behind fences in large enclosures. Next to them are two cheetahs, Jolly and Juba, lying peacefully on the grass. I greet each one by name, although they never seem to notice. A serval looks at me as I walk past from the windowsill in one of the adjacent bedrooms. As part of the wild cat breeding programme, he and his siblings are being looked after by another volunteer. I pass birds, rabbits, duikers and bushbucks—small antelope deemed safe enough to roam freely around the rehabilitation centre. Some mornings, Tiffany, a grey duiker, runs up behind me and gently butts me with her nose. Sometimes, if I am lucky, she lets me pet her, more curious about my camera. I talk to her for a few moments as she munches on whatever vegetation has taken her fancy.

Over gravelled pathways winding through lawns, animal enclosures and small buildings, I make my way to the meat room. Volunteers busy themselves in front, preoccupied with filling bowls in the trough-like sinks that line the wall outside. Inside the meat room, with a stainless-steel table occupying most of the space, I pick up two plastic bowls and fill them indifferently with the contents of a black bin bag on the floor. My mind wanders back to my first day, following my roommate's instructions on the day's tasks. Most nonchalantly, Susan had asked me to pass her some the bag's contents. Rooted to the spot, and nausea curdling inside my belly, I blinked several times, not quite comprehending what my eyes were seeing. Dozens of frozen, day-old chicks lay piled on top of each other; their lives snuffed out before they had a chance to live. I somehow found the will to reach down, freeing twelve of them from their icy bedchamber. The feel of the frozen hardness of death in my hand made me want to place each one protectively against my chest, but equally I wished to free my hand from this slippery cold being. The initial sight of these chicks brought back memories I have spent twenty years striving to forget; horrific scenes of slaughterhouses in a documentary I stumbled upon in my teens. Such was the impact that I chose not to eat meat from that moment on.

Paying scarce attention to the chicks defrosting in the bowl I carry around with me, I visit Dudu, a southern ground-hornbill. A sizeable bird, his long, thick, downward-curving beak with a small casque on the top makes me wary of getting too close. The striking red skin on his face and throat contrasts with his deep black plumage. Framing his inquisitive eyes are long, black lashes—the type a woman would die for. The reverberating boom of his call matches his name perfectly. I leave a few chicks around his enclosure for him to eat at his leisure.

In an adjacent enclosure are ten raptors with powerful hooked beaks and strong curved talons. These birds of prey sit next to each other, six feet off the ground, on a pole spanning the width of their enclosure. I hardly recognise myself now, striding confidently towards the birds, ensuring that the African fish eagle gets his fair share of the food. I chuckle to myself recalling the first time I stepped inside. Susan explained that I must place a chick on the pole next to each bird. Blinking in quick succession, I searched her face for signs that this was a joke and that she was daring me to do something both incredibly dangerous and stupid. Would these birds not peck my eyes out if I came too close? Nothing in her expression indicated that what she wanted me to do was out of the ordinary.

Gingerly I approached the birds, sitting in a row, towering above my head, watching my every move. I reached up to place a chick on the pole and primed myself for any sign of attack. The birds were still. I looked over my shoulder to check that Susan was not about to burst into laughter at my impending stupidity, but she was busying herself with cleaning. Stepping back a few feet to put some space between these towering beacons of power and myself, I waited. The black-chested snake eagle was the first to pin the chick to the pole with his talons and pull at the flesh with his beak. Upon realisation that I had been holding my breath for quite some time, I exhaled with relief.

Now, I return to the meat room for the remaining chicks that I left defrosting, hardly noticing the large stainless steel bowls filled with hunks of meat. With a sharp knife, I slice open the belly of each chick to remove the yolk. From experience, I know to stand slightly aside to avoid the putrid yellow liquid from splattering over my clothes, the stench of which never ceases to make me gag. There will not be time to change my clothes for a good few hours yet. To make it even easier for the orphaned baby pearl-spotted owls to eat, I cut off the head and deskin the lifeless body deftly and expertly, but with the utmost of respect.

These owls now fed, I turn my attention to a young orphaned African wood-owl named Trinity, also housed at the clinic. As I open the cage door, she looks at me with large dark eyes outlined by white eyebrows. I stroke the soft, downy feathers on her head with extra gentleness to avoid alarming her. As she closes her eyes, she chirps with each tender stroke. I respond to her chirping over the course of several minutes with soothing words as my heart melts. I am overcome by her vulnerability and her trust that I will cause her no harm.

With the owls now cared for, I head towards another enclosure, passing the vultures. Only the day before, a lappet-faced vulture swooped down onto my leather-gloved arm and ate chunks of meat from my hand. There is a lightness in my steps now for this is my favourite part of the day. A glorious creature of mesmerising beauty jumps up to greet me. As instructed, I turn my back to discourage this behaviour and tap him gently on the nose, but he quickly settles. While picking up his black sticky poo, Bullet, a one-year-old cheetah, follows beside me. Taken from his mother as a cub and hand-reared by staff, Bullet is accustomed to humans. To fulfil his job as 'species ambassador', he accompanies his handler to nearby farms and schools, educating adults and children alike on the urgency of saving this endangered species.

Now that Bullet's curiosity has been satisfied, he lays down on the grass between two trees, which shade him from the hot morning sun. His water bowl filled and enclosure cleaned, I sit down behind him on the earthy ground, my legs bent to one side. Stroking him as I would any house cat, his fur is coarse to the touch and his tail swishes as he purrs. I caress him gently, telling him that he is the most beautiful creature I have ever seen. He lifts his head and looks at me with his haunting amber eyes as if to tell me that he understands my every word. He places his head back down and I lay my hand on his side, feeling the heat of his body and the reverberations of his purring.

It was decades ago that I heard a female cheetah call to her cubs sequestered in a safe place in the grasses of the savannah. In the era before watch-on-demand TV, I caught a glimpse of this cheetah on a termite mound, her chirping pulling strings in my heart as Sir Attenborough smoothly relayed meticulously researched facts. Completely absorbed by the scene unfolding before me, it was the beginning of my fascination with the fastest land animal.

My mind wanders to Bandit and how she might be doing back home. A twinge of guilt results in a heavy sigh, but Bullet's purring snaps me out of a place my mind does not wish to go. I look around me, still stroking him absentmindedly. Men are fixing fences, volunteers walk purposefully with tools in hand, dassies that look like overgrown hamsters scamper through the grass, and secretary birds and marabou storks swoop down and fly off as they please. A group on the educational tour gaze at me curiously as they walk past, Bullet now lifting his head to look at them too. He puts his head back down seeing nothing of interest. I smile back, unsure if they decide that I must be brave or lucky to be so close to such a wild creature. I breathe in deeply—and quite involuntarily—as if an outside force is willing me to do so. As I exhale, it is as though I am in a dreamlike state, as if someone needs to pinch me, for where I am seems otherworldly, and so far removed from the world I know. I blink a few times, certain that this action will wake me from the most wonderful dream I have ever had, but I do not wake. For the first time in a long time, I am truly awake.

It will not be long before another volunteer takes my place as "sitter". Until then, I relish the privilege of such an encounter between two unlikely friends. I have yet to shake off the fogginess of my melancholy, comparable to the aftermath of a lingering anaesthetic. Still, Bullet's eyes blow gentle winds of hope, encouraging the tired edges of my life to ease. Whispering to Bullet as he sleeps, the creaking of the enclosure door makes me look up. I smile widely as Daniel, another volunteer, walks slowly towards me, his professional camera bag slung over his shoulder. In three swift movements, his camera is primed to capture what he sees before him. Normally I would have protested, loathing to see myself in photographs, but this time I do not, remembering that there is no longer any need to pose a certain way to avoid a profile shot. Unobtrusively, Daniel moves around me, the shutter clicking in quick succession. After a few minutes, he kneels beside me. Bullet remains asleep, his purrs still reverberating under my hand as I gaze down at the screen of Daniel's digital camera. I cannot believe my eyes. There I am, in South Africa, dressed in a dusty brown t-shirt, my hair pulled back off my face, sitting calmly behind a sleepy cheetah stretched out on the ground—the picture from my vision board brought to life.

At 8.30 a.m., we stop our chores. It is a ten-minute walk to Forest Camp, the luxurious tourist lodge of ten chalets overlooking the Quinine forest. The clouds hang low over the Mariepskop Mountains as we traverse through lush rainforest, over narrow streams and rocks, and sometimes through muddy terrain. Falling a little behind the twenty or so volunteers making their way to breakfast, I wish to walk alongside Dela, an orphaned one-year-old black rhino. Found stuck in a mud wallow in Kruger National Park a year earlier, she was hand-reared by the staff at Moholoholo and now has human companionship throughout the day. How quickly I have become used to these otherwise unusual experiences. Walking beside this magnificent beast, an animal so utterly trusting of her human companions, somehow feels wholly natural. Placing my hand gently on her back, her rough skin feels so different to that of my friend Bullet with his amber eyes. I respond conversationally to her occasional snorting, imagining what she might be saying, at the same time wishing our walk could last forever. A buffet-style breakfast of eggs, cereals, toast and jam is laid out for us under a large thatched-reed hut. Dela's pining, like the sound of air escaping out of a neck of a balloon, is a source of amusement, as she pokes her head through one of the glassless windows.

Over the course of the rest of the day, I tend to other animals. Two servals enjoy chasing a stick that I slither along the grass. Although Scruffball often hides, Emma rubs her body against my legs encouraging me to stay a while longer. Close by are two adult pearl-spotted owls, perched on a wooden stick. What should be a simple task of placing chicks on their perch causes me a great deal of torment. There are two doors to open, a safety feature to prevent the owls from escaping. There, in the small space between the two metal, ring-fenced doors, are countless spiders. It is a test for my severe arachnophobia. On the days that Susan is with me, she feeds these owls without me. On the days that I am alone, I make use of my rake. The spiders have two choices—scuttle away or be crushed.

In the afternoons, I feed the bush baby. These "little night monkeys" are arboreal and nocturnal, related to the lemurs of Madagascar and about the size of a squirrel. I adore his bat-like ears, distinctive forward-facing eyes which are oversized in relation to his head, and his long tail that wraps around my arm as he clings to me. Unable to move his eyes in their sockets, I marvel at the way he can look directly backwards. He climbs onto my shoulder and wraps his arms around my neck; his silver-grey fur is soft and his human-like hands are surprisingly cool against my skin. There are also two genets to feed. These cat-like animals with slender bodies and a long ringed tail have no problem pouncing onto my head from their perch or running up my leg. Playing with them awhile, the antics of an animal I have never seen or heard of before fascinate me.

Back in my room, Susan introduces me to four hungry dormice in a cage waiting for their next meal. Friends of one of the staff members, on holiday for a week, requested that these rodents stay at Moholoholo. Assigned their care, Susan has brought frozen insects from the fridge at the clinic. Looking around our room for additional sustenance, I glance over to the open windows that invariably allow insects inside. Moths, attracted to the light outside now cling to the greyish net curtain, their dark form easily discernible. Gently cupping one in my hand, I bring it to outstretched paws that grab the unfortunate creature.

The afternoons are always a time of rest. It is a time to escape the sun that makes my skin sticky or the rain that pours down, sometimes non-stop for two days, covering my trousers in mud as I squelch my way over the grass. When I remember, I don my wet gear, even though it is more unflattering than my uniform. I often poke my head into the girls' bedrooms to chat with my fellow volunteers. As we are similar in age, I enjoy Courtney's company the most. From the United States, she has a fascinating background, even raising an orphaned kangaroo in her own home. Deep in conversation on her bed, sometimes Dela barges in, preferring to be naughty rather than stay with the volunteer assigned to keep her company. All we can do is laugh and get out of her way while she knocks over the side lamps, stands on the beds and wreaks havoc. Her antics make for great storytelling over dinner.

The afternoon is also a time to be alone for a few hours. It is odd to find myself in the company of others night and day, and although my busy, purpose-filled days nurture me, I sometimes long for some solitude. I lay on my bed, cocooned by the mosquito net and think back to my second day, only two weeks ago. Lunch was ready in the common room, laid out for us in plastic containers on the brown L-shaped countertop. An Australian volunteer called Jenny and I were the first to arrive. A few old white ceiling fans moved the warm air through the large room of wooden tables and chairs arranged in a seating of four and six. A large oversized, leafy patterned, wooden-framed couch and four matching armchairs were arranged along one wall.

Darren, a staff member and Dela's primary caregiver, leaned against the cupboards of the L-shaped kitchen waiting to greet the newest volunteers. Nineteen and boyishly handsome, he engaged Jenny, half my age, in intense conversation. Naturally pretty with a long dark-brown ponytail pushed through the back of her navy baseball cap, she exuded an air that butter would not melt in her mouth. However, underneath lay an unkindness that she would inflict on all who would irritate her. With no one else in the room, I felt like a third wheel as neither Jenny nor Darren concealed their mutual attraction. There was a time when I used to turn heads, but now I carry an air of weariness, worn down by facing life's challenges alone. As I looked on, I felt old and invisible, not helped by the baggy, oversized beige uniform. Busying myself with the decision about what to eat until other volunteers finally walked in, distracted me from the sudden and acute pain in my heart. It was a shocking reminder of the emptiness of my life—a life that, in moments like this, felt lost, wasted and unfulfilled.

Other volunteers now filled the room, most I had met in the first twenty-four hours. A volunteer I had not seen before strode up to me, pinning me with a clear, penetrating, gaze. His piercing marine-blue eyes that change colour, sometimes shifting to shades of green and grey depending on the light, settled on the deep and lustrous darkness of mine. Daniel told me he had planned to be in Africa for six weeks. He was staying at Moholoholo for a few weeks, but was undecided about where he would go after that. He had just lost his job as an IT professional, and was taking some time out to recharge his batteries. His carefree attitude intrigued me, allowing his adventure to unfold as it pleased. Six-foot-three with honey-blond hair, his Dutch accent sounded like the softness of melting toffee.

Did I really have to fly six thousand miles just to meet someone who could walk alongside me through life, saving me from enduring it alone, someone who could be more than just a fleeting encounter? What a story that would make. A chance meeting, so unconventional and uncontrived, so serendipitous, rendering internet dating utterly lacking in depth or imagination. He told me his surname, which was remarkably Jewish-sounding. He told me about the summer he spent on a Kibbutz in Israel and of his plans to meet up with a friend he had met there during this trip to South Africa. Marrying outside my faith would be out of the question and would make my life immeasurably more difficult. Not religious, but grounded in my upbringing, a Jewish partner is what I want—not because I am told that this should be so, but because I am inextricably linked to my Jewish identity and with that comes a way of life. It is challenging enough when both partners are of the same faith, and even more so when they are not. Without being too obvious, I tried to ascertain if he was Jewish. It soon became evident that he was not. Of course not. Coincidental happenstances leading to life partners are for Hollywood movies and other people.

The number of volunteers changes from week to week, so some days there is less to do. On one of these days with nothing particularly pressing, I find Brian in his office. As the rehabilitation centre manager for twenty years now, his experience with animals is legendary. Four decades ago, as a young game ranger, he was part of the first team to relocate rhinos to South Africa's flagship Kruger National Park. Staff members and volunteers alike revere his knowledge of the bush, which spans nearly six decades. To hundreds of schoolchildren, tourists, and veterinary students he is a much-loved teacher. On most days, he calls to Big Boy, the lion he rescued seventeen years earlier from someone keeping him illegally as a pet. Sadly, Big Boy's sisters had died of malnourishment. In the early days, he roamed free around Moholoholo with Brian by his side. Too big for such freedom now, he spends his days in a large grassy enclosure with a lioness called Ditch. I have only heard Big Boy's roars in the distance as I do my rounds or late into the night. Now I wish to witness this renowned bond between man and lion for myself. We arrange a time to meet the next day.

As I walk to meet Brian, I feel joyous and grateful having just come from sitting with Bullet and tending to the animals in my care. Not splattering my clothes with rank yellow yolk this particular morning pleased me and the spiders were surprisingly absent around the spotted-owl enclosure. While I am excited to witness Big Boy roar with my own eyes, my expectation is that the experience will be fascinating but over within a few minutes, so I have plans to meet Daniel in the common room in just half an hour. He will be waiting there to show me his pictures from his bush walk the day before. On this particular day, I feel balanced, on an even keel, centred.

Brian comes out from behind his desk, which is groaning under the weight of piles of papers. His uniform is off-white trousers and matching half-sleeved shirt, and he never goes anywhere without his greyish Tilly hat. I thank him for giving up his time, knowing that he is a very busy man. We chat as we walk the short distance towards Big Boy's enclosure, where we find the lion outstretched on the grass beside Ditch. Brian instructs me to stand close to the fence, while he stands about thirty feet behind me. I wait, not knowing what to expect. In a booming voice, Brian calls out, "Big Boy, Big Boy". Upon hearing his name, Big Boy stands up. I smile at this response, of Big Boy's recognition of his own name and of Brian's voice, but my mind is still on Daniel waiting for me. Brian calls his name again and this time Big Boy roars strong and loud, throwing his head back as he does. Suddenly, the familiar feeling of upset washes over me. Blinking rapidly to fight back the tears, this sudden rush of emotion takes me unawares. Motionless and frozen to the spot, I stare at Big Boy, his full mane framing his magnificent face in all his lion glory. Unable to move, I push down yet another lump in my throat. Again and again, Brian calls out his name, Big Boy roaring in response, louder each time. Ditch is now on her feet, roaring in unison. Powerless to stop the wave of emotion that has suddenly engulfed me, the primal sounds of these majestic beasts continue, reverberating against the trees, against every fibre of my being. Involuntarily, I fall to the ground, clutching the grass in an attempt to steady my body from the uncontrollable shaking. Bent over with my forehead almost touching the grass, my heaving sobs are unrestrainable. The air is too thick to swallow. I can barely breathe. The calls and roars continue for yet another few minutes as my cries ring out from a place deep from within, a place that I have never been to before.

Big Boy's roars play out in front of me like a storybook unfolding—seen not with my eyes, but with my heart. Each roar is a liberating scream that strikes me with the impact of all that he is feeling, of his life story, and the message he is so desperate for me and for the world to hear. With each roar, I feel his eternal love for Brian who saved him from a life of unimaginable horror. I feel his gratitude for his safe enclosure, but also his resignation of the circumstances that led to his captivity in the first place. I feel his frustration of not being free, out in the wilderness and living how lions are supposed to live, master of all they survey, king of kings. In his roar, I hear his desperate cry for the world to end the madness, to end the destruction of beast and land, the senseless killing of his species, and all species inextricably linked to his. Each roar punches me with a thud, rattling the armour I have spent decades creating to protect myself from the outside world. Each roar squeezes my heart, trying to dislodge years of anguish and hurt. My tears, as they fall on the grass below, wring with inner pain, both his and mine. He wills me to listen. Brian finally walks away unperturbed. This is not the first time he has seen such a reaction. For half an hour more, still unable to move, waves of unfettered emotion render me completely incapacitated.

My sobbing now finally abating, I run back to my room, hoping that no one will see me. My hair plastered over my face and bloodshot eyes can only mean one thing. Throwing open the bedroom door, Susan looks up from drawing a sketch of one of the genets from the comfort of her bed. "Is it a good cry or bad cry?" she asks. Somehow, I manage to say "good" but in reality, I do not know. I shower in the hope that the cascading water will wash away whatever has just happened to me. Another bout of sobbing grips me and my tears mix with the water pummelling me. At dinnertime, I am subdued. Other volunteers ask me how my day has been, but all I can muster is a forced response of "fine". Exhausted, I sit silently amongst the din of chatter, present in body but not in mind. Daniel sits beside me and takes my hand. He leans over and whispers, "You can tell me in your own time."

Later, in the coolness of the night air, Daniel sits next to me on a bench outside the common room. He knows something must have happened for me not to meet up with him that afternoon. His hand engulfs mine, and we look out into the black night beyond. I dare not look into his eyes for fear that he will see the tears that refuse to remain in check. "Whatever it is, you can tell me," he says softly. Through half sentences and a jumble of details that I am sure are not making sense, I tell him what happened that afternoon, stuffing down my rising emotion. Leaning forward, I look at the ground and stare at an ant making its way past. My shoulders are hunched and my lips quiver as I speak. Daniel has been looking at me all this time, gazing softly with his kind eyes that I cannot see. Still holding my hand he says, "The feelings you have for animals are beautiful, a rare quality that you must hold on to, no matter what anyone says. Your heart is too big for you sometimes." Now I turn to him, his smile undoing all my resolve. Crying softly, he holds me until my body stops shaking. Exhausted from the day's rollercoaster of emotion, I fall asleep with my head resting against his shoulder. A couple of hours later, Daniel picks me up and carries me to my room. Half asleep, I slip into bed without undressing.

In the days that follow, I cry at the least thought of Big Boy and his roars, withholding tears until I find a private place to unleash them. I start to wonder if there is something wrong with me. I think back to the dead chicks in the plastic bag, to the dead animals behind the clinic for distribution to the predators, and to the film showing an entire elephant herd being shot from a helicopter in the name of conservation. While incredibly upsetting, jarring, and at times shocking, none of these experiences affected me so forcefully. As hard as I try, the experience with Big Boy will not leave my mind. There must be a reason, a simple or not-so-simple explanation. Desperate for answers but equally hesitant to ask, I do not want to be seen as overly emotional or a crybaby from the city unable to handle the complexities of conservation. Tentatively, I approach Lisa, the same staff member who welcomed me the first day, whose gentleness and sensitivity contrasts to the macho demeanour of some of her male colleagues. While she is sympathetic and respectfully acknowledges the tears that are threatening to come as I recount the story, she cannot offer any explanation other than "it just happens sometimes". This provides no comfort to me.

The following day, I go about my rounds as usual, but Big Boy's roars never leave my mind. Albeit temporarily, one incident *does* make me forget all about it. In an enclosure next to Big Boy is a lioness whose name I do not know. I do not think she even has a name. A snare severely damaged her back foot and now Moholoholo is her home. She is an angry lioness and I do not blame her, her life now in captivity. My task is simple: fill her water bowl inside her enclosure from the tap *outside* the fence. I dismiss warnings that she may charge at me. What is there to worry about? I walk up to her enclosure and see her ears poking out of the long grass at the far end. The rangers have told us that this lioness is capable of jumping the fence with enough motivation. Therefore, a second fence surrounds the first, making a walkway between the two. To turn on the tap, I first enter the walkway. Doing so, I quickly position myself behind the feeding cage and check where she is. From there, I simply have to walk a few feet along the fence and turn on the tap.

If the lioness charges, she will scare me more than I have ever been in my life. She cannot reach me, but I find myself trying to figure out a way to avoid her seeing me. I tell myself not to be stupid. Staff and volunteers do this every day. I just need to turn on the tap and walk away. I pluck up enough courage to walk past the feeding cage and get on my tippy toes to see above the tall grass. Her ears are still visible. She is definitely much nearer now but still far enough away that I can turn on the tap and then hide behind the feeding cage if necessary. Utterly ridiculous, scared of a lioness on the other side of a fence. Praying that she does not come closer before it is time to turn off the tap, I walk a little further to turn it on. Again, I glance in her direction to check where she is. I can still see her ears, but she has moved closer yet again.

Glancing back and forth from the bowl to the yellow ears peeking out from the grass, I try to calculate the time it will take for the bowl to fill. Satisfied that there is enough fresh water in the bowl, I turn off the tap. Big Boy lets out a deep growl in my direction from the adjacent enclosure, making me jump. Hurriedly, I walk away and open the gate leading out of the walkway. My shaking hands fumble with the padlock. With the job done, I lean against the fence and take a deep breath to steady my pounding heart. The adrenaline lasts for a few hours more. For the first time in a long time, I feel alive.

As it is my turn for aviary duty one particular morning, I am up before most of the other volunteers and revel in the stillness of sunrise. On my way there, a sharp searing pain down the left side of my body stops me in my tracks. Frantically, I run my hands over my upper body and head to rid myself of whatever has caused me this pain. Mentally running through a list of what could have bitten me, I rule out a mosquito. Maybe it was a spider. That thought makes me shudder. Could it have been a boomslang? We were warned about this poisonous arboreal snake whose venom packs a deadly punch. Just a few days earlier, we found one in the girls' dorm room. Six of us joined a game ranger in a pickup truck, the snake in a cloth bag dangling on the outside of the truck for its release in the Limpopo Reserve. However, as we neared the gates, the snake escaped through a hole at the bottom of the bag and slithered away. We laughed but sworn to secrecy. The mere mention of the word *snake* leaves one particular volunteer incapacitated. It could not have been a boomslang because I was not particularly close to any trees. The fiery pain is not passing and I am more than concerned.

For five minutes, I am rooted to the spot, gripping my shoulder. To my right is Brian's house. If the pain does not subside within a few minutes, I will knock on his door. It is still early in the morning, so I am hesitant to wake a sleeping household for what could very well be insignificant. With nothing but a sequence of deep, steadying breaths, I ride out the pain. As it eventually begins to subside, I continue my path to the aviary. The first wooden door creaks as it opens and closes behind me. The second door creaks seconds later. The room is small with a countertop on one side and metal shelving on the opposite wall, stacked high with plastic containers of supplies. Here I find Sally, a five-foot-nothing Yorkshire lass, with short, straight blonde hair scooping the seeds out of a dozen papaya. She is cutting the sweet orange flesh, dividing it among several plates for different parts of the aviary. I liked Sally from the moment I met her. She is down to earth, funny with a heart of gold. She confided in me that she was rather homesick, having never left her hometown before. I was therefore disappointed to overhear Jenny teasing her about nothing in particular, especially when I saw the hurt in Sally's eyes. In a quiet moment, I told her she could hang out with me and sit beside me at meal times.

Feigning calmness, I ask her to check my shoulder for signs of a bite or any other wound. She only sees a small red dot. I am reassured. I am relieved too that now, less than an hour later, the pain is completely absent. Taking a couple of plates of papaya, we step out of the little room and into the aviary, bending over to get through a hatch at the bottom of the door, a safety measure to prevent the birds from escaping. The din of dozens of mating pairs of birds of countless colours and sizes never ceases to please me. They flit from branch to branch, from one feeding perch to another, singing and chirping. It is warm inside, similar to that of a greenhouse, but not oppressive. I look up at the birds on the upper foliage. Standing like this, just beneath the wire fencing, reminds me of their captivity. I place a couple of plates at the far end of the aviary, beside water tables and thick foliage that guide me through a labyrinth of winding pathways. At lunch, I relay the incident of my mysterious pain, which was a newsworthy story to me, to a couple of game rangers. They tell me that if I was not bleeding, dying or losing my arm, then I was OK. I walk away feeling foolish for even mentioning it.

Weekly trips to the nearby town of Hoedspruit provide a welcome break from the daily chores and serve as a pick-up point for arriving volunteers. The modern café allows me to indulge in a delicious coffee and enjoy the buzz of a small town. I motion for one of the new volunteers to join me at my table—I know how daunting the first couple of days here can be. Jane is from the UK and vegetarian, and I am delighted that we have something in common. Over coffee, she tells me that Brian has granted her special permission. This prompts me to ask her what exactly her exemption is. "Not look at meat," she says. In surprise, I look up from the half-eaten cake on my plate. This must be some sort of mistake. Meat is everywhere. Almost all of the rounds involve meat of some kind. What is she going to do then? As a non-meat eater, I fully understand the reasons why one becomes a vegetarian, but if the look of meat is so offensive, why come to a wildlife reserve where feeding meat to carnivores is a daily occurrence? Freshly killed cows or impala behind the clinic, their blood draining down the pathway in advance of dismemberment are sights that are initially hard to stomach. So too are large stainless steel trays filled with hunks of beef in the meat room or on the back of a pickup truck along with hundreds of bones of dead animals for the vultures, but that is the reality of life at this rehabilitation centre.

Since my arrival, there has been no choice but to come to terms with the gritty, unpleasant side of conservation, with sights that made me want to be sick, cry or scream. I did not ask for special dispensation. Working outside in the heat is difficult at times, made increasingly challenging when some volunteers do not pull their weight, simply wanting to check their reflection in any shiny surface. Sometimes after we complete the mandatory tasks, we assist with additional but optional chores. It is always the same few volunteers who offer up their time—including Daniel and I. Utterly confused at what Jane has just told me, my irritation turns to visible annoyance. Daniel, glancing sharply from the other side of the table, silently warns me to mind my own business.

In the days that follow, Jane takes over the task of sitting with a sick, orphaned young sable, who, despite everybody's best efforts, does not make it. I have barely seen Jane since she arrived, so I was surprised when she joined us at the feeding cages. We spend a lot of time cleaning out these cages inside the lion and cheetah enclosures. A series of pulleys open and close the guillotine-style metal doors leading from the cage to the enclosure and into the cage from the outside. Once fed, the cats are free to roam about their enclosure, leaving us to remove bones and clean the blood left behind. Much to my annoyance, my arachnophobia somehow allows me to see spiders others would never notice. My broom proves to be a handy and trusty weapon. In groups of four, we work quickly, taking over from one another when the exertion in the heat becomes too arduous. After twenty minutes of repetitive scrubbing and rinsing, the cage is finally clean. There are another four to do. Jane cries as she scrubs the congealed blood off the metal floor. Instead of sympathetic gestures and words of understanding from my fellow volunteers, there are rolling eyes and half-concealed snickers. I walk away, uninterested.

Two weeks in, my volunteer companions begin to feel more like a family. However, the childish behaviour of the younger volunteers, who like to keep a seat for their newest best friend, rankles me and is a painful reminder of my school days. Although, more recently, no matter where I sit, Daniel sits beside me at a chair often purposely left empty by those who have seen the furtive glances and the strength of our growing friendship. He is also uninterested in the trivial conversation of my younger counterparts who continuously compete for attention from the all-male game rangers. He tells me of his trip to the Phi Phi Islands of Thailand, a brief teaching job in China, and the Indian Ocean tsunami he narrowly escaped while in Indonesia in 2004. He tells me of his dreams to become a remote operator vehicle pilot, a small submersible craft that performs underwater exploration, and of his plans to pass Cisco IT exams. Above all, he dreams of owning a reserve in Southern Africa to make a lasting difference to wildlife and local communities.

Daniel had originally planned to spend time in Uganda among the gorillas but chose Moholoholo at the last moment. Inexplicably, he is drawn to Africa; its wildness reflects his yearning to be free, to be disentangled from a life of "metro-boulot-dodo", a French expression that loosely translates as "the rat race". He is torn between a life that is now only a pipe dream and a life he knows he must return to—one of job hunting, his friends, his parents and siblings, especially his brother who he talks to every day. We talk of returning to Africa together, climbing Kilimanjaro and living a life immersed in nature, far from the humdrum and the daily grind of the lives we left behind. This prospect seems more palatable to me than returning to a life I have not yet laid out for myself. I indulge in my fantasy for a few minutes more but I know that my return to reality will be upon me all too soon.

One evening over dinner, he whispers to me to meet him outside my bedroom door at midnight, but he refuses to tell me why. I glance at the others to check if anyone has overheard. Relationships between volunteers are not permitted. While I completely understand this rule, probably borne out of an unwanted pregnancy of an eighteen-year-old teenager, free from the confines of her family for the first time, I am not a teenager, nor do I believe that rules, especially this one, apply to me. Seven years of strict uniform policies enforced by the prefects at my secondary school—to close the top button of my red shirt, fix my red and navy tie in a neat snug fitting knot, and pull my knee-length socks all the way up—was the beginning of my dislike of rules, and the belief that they were mostly for other people. However, once I became a prefect, I too enforced those same infernal rules.

Barely able to contain my excitement, I slip into bed at 9 p.m., still fully clothed. Susan does not notice—she is in the throes of telling me how much she misses her boyfriend back in England and of their plans to get married. Tall and lean, she is a professional photographer, her creativity evident in the images she captures in colour, black and white, and sepia, each one more stunning than the last. She is unquestionably talented, but entirely humble and unassuming when she shows us the growing number of sketches filling her oversized scrapbook. I sleep for a while but wake up shortly before midnight. Susan remains fast asleep. Daniel whispers my name through the open bedroom window. The wooden door squeaks and my eyes glance over to Susan's bed. She does not stir. Daniel's presence outside my room would certainly get us both into trouble. The night air is cool and I am glad of my jumper. He takes my hand and whispers that he wants to take me to a special place. Unbeknownst to me, for the last few days, he has been searching for a place where we can be together, away from prying eyes.

There is no moon this particular night and no lights to guide our way. Barely able to see what is in front of me and walking almost blind through the darkness, I put out my left hand to feel my way. This same route, familiar during daylight hours is now utterly unfamiliar. With every step, my apprehension rises. I am very scared of the dark, a fear most likely rooted in a burglary at home that occurred through an upstairs window while my parents were entertaining downstairs. I was the first to discover the crime. Entering a dark room without immediately locating the light switch causes me consternation. Daniel assures me that he knows the way. I tell him that I think it would be better to turn back, but we carry on. There is no choice but to put my complete trust in him. I am well aware that we are breaking the rules. If caught, we would most certainly be asked to leave, but the thrill of walking blindly through the darkness with a man who is as gentle as a sea breeze and as rebellious as a captured wild horse is far too exciting for me to abandon. Daniel guides me up the creaky wooden steps of the viewing platform, our rustling and hushed whispers prompting a soft grunting from Chui the leopard and low rumblings from Big Boy in their enclosures below, adding to my exhilaration.

Laying on our backs, we look up. It is the first time since my arrival that I have made a conscious effort to look up at the night sky. With no artificial light, the glory of the stars is unimpeded. Reminding Daniel yet again that we are breaking the rules, he tells me that he does not care, believing that rules are for other people. We laugh at how similar we are in so many ways, our rejection of social norms, and of needing to be free spirits, unshackled by life's demands. My body relaxes more deeply, although the wooden platform still feels too hard against my back. To take my mind off it, I ask Daniel to speak to me in Dutch. My mangled repetition of a simple sentence makes me giggle. Foreign languages intrigue me. I enjoy how the newness of unfamiliar words feel in my mouth and the sound of them in my ears, each word granting me access to a new world, enriching mine. Laying my head upon his chest, allowing my breathing to match his, the warmth of his hand reminds me how long I have endured the acute physical and emotional pain that comes with the sustained absence of intimacy. Daniel nuzzles my neck, his breath hot in comparison to the cool night air. As the hours pass, we are grateful that the bullfrogs, hyenas, crickets, cicadas and the abundant nocturnal life have chosen to be particularly raucous. Leading me safely back to my room, Daniel kisses me softly and I fall into bed with just enough time for a couple of hours of sleep before my alarm rouses me for another day.

Now, over two weeks into my stay, and comfortable with the routine here at Moholoholo, I find myself eager to experience something a little different. I jump at the opportunity to join in on a bush walk the following day at Nhoveni, a privately owned part of Kruger National Park. My alarm jolts me at 4.30 a.m. on the morning of the walk. I have hardly slept, kept awake by a party in the common room that continued until the early morning hours. Functioning on only a few hours' sleep is always a challenge for me. Casting aside my displeasure, I turn on my headlamp so as not to wake Susan. Instinctively, I scan the room for insects. There is a spider on the ceiling, but it is quite small and on the other side of the room, so it is not an immediate concern. There is no time to take care of it anyway. The bathroom reveals a small cockroach under the sink. It meets its end at the back of a shoe. No spiders in the shower today. Once outside my bedroom, I reach for my boots, automatically shaking them out as if this has been part of my daily routine for years. I try to put it out of my mind that it is still dark outside and that the meeting place in front of the gates is a few minutes' walk away. How different my life is here; walking alone in the dark at 5 a.m. is completely unheard of in my real life.

Four of us, including Jenny, Stephanie, and Kelly, a red-headed South African trainee vet with charming freckles, climb into the Mahindra, a green safari game drive vehicle with grilled sides and a canvas roof. It will take an hour to get to Nhoveni. The wind batters my face as we speed along. My head is down, and one hand on my hat is preventing it from blowing away. Kelly and Jenny have had the foresight to bring a blanket—lucky for them. My travel sickness pills have yet to kick in and the idea of vomiting in front of the others is alarming. I try to allow the motion of the vehicle to lull me to sleep but insects fly into my face, smarting as they smack my cheeks at full speed. I keep my mouth closed. The pills start to work just as we turn off the highway and onto a bumpy dirt road that will take us to the camp.

After a short while, we stop in what feels like the middle of nowhere. There is nothing for miles around. Our bush walk starts here—my first. Accompanied by three game rangers, we meet up with Brian. All carry rifles. We walk in single file, with rangers at the front and back. Brian says that if he tells us to run, we must do so as if our lives depend on it, but what animal could I possibly outrun? Concluding that he is only trying to scare us unnecessarily to add to the excitement and trepidation of an experience so far removed from what any of us have experienced before, the rumble of a lion in the distance and the reality of my situation start to sink in. Out here in the bush, we are unprotected against the wildlife who, despite their cuteness in pictures, are indeed ferocious. Brian relays a story of how a leopard killed a game ranger as he stood on guard on the lookout for poachers. Glancing furtively from side to side, through the trees and into the distance in an attempt to catch a glimpse of any impending danger, my legs feel wobbly and I trip over small stones, only slightly comforted by the rifles slung over the shoulders of the men accompanying us.

We walk along the empty riverbed, slightly damp from all the rain over the past few days. Brian asks us to identify the animal tracks as we walk along. Some are easy to decipher, others more difficult. How can you tell the difference between kudu or nyala antelope? Male or female? Tracking is a language I have yet to learn. Elephant tracks that trail off into the distance leave deep oval imprints on the sand. The hand and footprints resembling those of humans are easily identifiable as those belonging to baboon. Prints with three toes belong to that of a black rhino since its heel has a shallow indentation, but it will take me some time before I can distinguish it from that of a white rhino. Lion tracks are unlikely to be mistaken given their large size, and the fact that these cats are highly social means there would usually be more than one set of tracks together. Cheetah prints are easier to identify with claw marks normally visible because it is the only cat to have semi-retractable claws. Thrilled that these magnificent creatures have passed this way, some only hours before, the apparent freshness of some leopard tracks, similar to those of a lion, but smaller, is concerning.

By 7 a.m., it is already unbearably hot. Although the sleeves of my t-shirt are rolled up and tucked in at the top, I now wish to be free of it entirely as it clings to my body in patches of sweat. A trickle of perspiration runs down my back. My throat is dry and scratchy, and the rumbling of my stomach is becoming harder to disguise. No one is carrying water since Brian said it would not be necessary for this part of the trip. Maybe it is not necessary for him because he is so accustomed to the climate, but now I wish I had not listened. Brian continuously asks the rangers to name the birds and plants we see—the common and scientific names. More often than not, the game rangers do not know. The names of the fauna and flora sound funny to me. I wish I had my notepad, as I will invariably forget within minutes. Brian knows the name of every bird and replicates many of their calls, which amuses and impresses me immensely. We continue walking on the sandy riverbed. A hand signal from Brian tells us to stop. He smells leopard. We sniff the air and nod in agreement, as if this is entirely obvious. I look up into the trees, expecting to see a leopard laying lazily among its branches. I have watched too many films it seems.

We walk a little further and encounter more elephant tracks. I would really like to see an elephant. This thought takes my mind off the leopard I want to see, but equally do not. I know if we see a leopard, we could very well be in too much danger. With the sun now higher in the sky, I am cursing not bringing water. My mind wanders to when we might eat, but the bird, plant and tracking lessons continue. Finally, we arrive at the lodge that accommodates students conducting research, but we do not go inside. Instead, at the top of a hill we sit at the viewing station, a round structure made of stones and small benches. The first sip of coffee, even though it is instant, tastes delicious. We eat sandwiches of egg, tuna and cucumber on fresh white bread. Great expanses of land stretch out for miles, with trees, bushes and grasses as far as the eyes can see. A large watering hole lies within easy sight but there are currently no animals drinking from it. This disappoints me. I would have been able to see them really well with my binoculars. I wait a little longer, scanning the landscape. It is void of buildings or any other manmade structures, clear terrain perfect to observe any creature wandering close to the watering hole. Nothing comes. Still, I feel like the luckiest girl alive.

We set off again at 10 a.m. in search of the "Big Five", a phrase coined by big-game hunters that refers to the five most difficult animals in Africa to hunt on foot: lion, leopard, buffalo, elephant and rhino. As we drive through open and then dense terrain, we spot zebra, wildebeest, giraffe, countless impala, a raucous troupe of baboons, two hippo, and a black-backed jackal bouncing along in the grass. Unfortunately, we do not see any predators or elephants, but my yearning to see wild animals in their natural environment has been satisfied. I am elated by the entire experience of seeing wild animals so close, living freely. If my trip were to end right at this moment, I would be altogether content.

As midday approaches, we drive back to the rustic lodge to escape the hottest part of the day. Exhausted from the early start and the heat, we each search for a place to sleep for a few hours. One volunteer finds a wooden table set in the middle of a courtyard, another a wooden bench. Both look incredibly uncomfortable. In one of the bedrooms, I flop down on the mattress but I am too tired to care that it is heavily stained. It looks as if no one has stayed here for quite some time. Sleep comes quickly and remains undisturbed until the sound of mosquitoes whizzing past my ears abruptly interrupts my slumber. The decision to remove my shoes and socks is costing me dearly now. Welts have started to form where mosquitoes have feasted on my ankles. Impossible to go back to sleep, I make my way over to an old cracked mirror hanging on the wall. An insect that had flown into my face earlier is still stuck there.

A few hours later, we drive back to Moholoholo. Again, I dip my head down to protect myself from the driving wind. While I would much rather change out of my dirty and sweaty clothes, there is no time for that before dinner.

I recount my delight at the wild animals I have seen, my nervousness at walking on the dry riverbed and my sheer exhaustion under the heat, but my senses have been on overload and my explanation of all the wondrous sights and sounds does not do it justice.

In my final week, I am hungry for another adrenaline-charged experience, one that I will not forget, and I do not have to wait long. A farmer had contacted Moholoholo relaying his intention to shoot a herd of hippos that had wandered onto his land. A game capture team set to work building a temporary enclosure to corral the herd. For the past few months, hippos have been wandering in and out of this boma. Once all the hippos are inside, the game capture team will close the gate and the hippos will be loaded into trucks and transported to another location. The team invites us to watch. I am rather nervous about this particular excursion having decided before I chose my destinations that I would not join a game capture project. I knew I could not bear to see animal relocation, even though it is for their own safety and wellbeing. The thought of people corralling animals into pens, cages, trucks or any such enclosure fills me with such unease, especially knowing that the animals would not comprehend what was happening to them. Of course, I had a choice not to witness the event, but I did not want to be the only one left behind. I reconciled that perhaps the process would not be quite as bad as I had imagined.

We leave at 7 p.m. The majority of the volunteers and game rangers set off in a large van, while Daniel and I, along with four others, take a smaller one. We drive for forty-five minutes. The game capture team has been at the location for hours already, guiding the hippos further into the boma and into the truck. We are not allowed to approach until all the large hippos are inside. If they were to ram the side of the metal pen at the entrance of the enclosure, they might get out. This would be disastrous. It is impossible to outrun a hippo. Instead, we are instructed to wait in the vans until we get the signal. It will be a long wait.

One of the game rangers comes to the window to reveal a firefly cupped in his hands, the yellow glow of its bioluminescence lighting up the darkness. It is the stuff of fairy tales, elusive—there one moment, gone the next. It flies off far too soon. The six of us are quieter now as the hours pass. Tired, cold and uncomfortable in the backseat, without light it is impossible to make out the time from my watch. I am even too tired to take my headlamp out of my pocket. I lean my head against the window and force myself to sleep, but the sound of mosquitoes buzzing in my ear makes sleeping very challenging. My last minute decision to change into long trousers and boots will at least give me some protection. My fleece is pulled over my face and my hands are in my pockets, but those pesky mosquitos find a way to bite me anyway. At 11 p.m., we get the signal to go to the boma. We drive very slowly in the darkness without headlights. The three rangers walking in front of the van resemble shadowy white ghosts under the moonlight.

Jumping out of the van, we walk a few hundred yards to the metal holding pen. All the hippos are in the truck except for two young females. They bellow. From outside the pen, men shout at the hippos to move up the ramp, guiding them with a light and an electric prod. Zap. Zap. Zap. I flinch and wonder how many volts it delivers. The prod does not touch the hippos—the sound of it against the metal bars is enough to make them move. Not knowing which way to turn, they go in circles, bellowing. We make our way closer to the pen, stepping over an electric wire low to the ground. If the hippos start ramming the side of the pen, they stand a good chance of escaping. If that happens, we would all have no choice but to run. How fast can I actually run? I would have to get over this electric wire. Doing this panicked in the dark would not exactly give me an advantage over a charging hippo.

The two female hippos grow increasingly distressed, bellowing and swaying from side to side, confused as to which way to go. One rams against the side of the pen. Collectively, we gasp and move back. Daniel takes my hand to steady me. I edge my way to the electric wire, just in case. I decide that if she rams the pen again, I will step back over the wire. The men are still shouting. Zap. Zap. Zap. The bellowing continues. The two hippos go up the ramp but are spooked and come back down. After several more attempts, they finally go into the truck. The sound of clanging doors, the shouting in an unfamiliar language, and the Zap Zap Zap is too stressful for me, and I cannot fathom what it must like for the hippos.

It is close to 1 a.m. when we get back to the vans and follow the truck to another reserve called Mountain View.

Once we arrive, the hippos will be unloaded into another boma. At Mountain View, a walkway several metres high overlooks the compartments of the boma, each with a metal door. Around twenty of us climb up a ladder and stand on the walkway. We must stand there in complete silence and the only torches allowed are those belonging to the game capture team. Not even our cameras are permitted.

The hippos are destined for different reserves and need to be separated, including the young from their mothers. From my position on the walkway high off the ground, there is a pen with a guillotine-style metal door on the right. One young male hippo runs down the ramp and rams into the side of the pen. The whole structure sways. Having poor eyesight, he bangs himself again against the side in an attempt to find a way out. The sides are made of plastic sheeting and will not cause him any harm. Immediately, he urinates and defecates, the smell of which reaches my nose quite unapologetically. Seeing his distress, my heart feels as if it is being ripped open. Hurtling down the ramp, his mother joins him a few minutes later. For now, they are reunited. Unable to see what is happening in the other pens, all I can hear is "kom, kom, kom" and the words for open and close in Afrikaans. The game capture team is having trouble opening and closing the metal door that screeches while they try to release it fully to the ground. The hippos are bellowing; like a dozen chainsaws in advance of the appalling destruction they are about to wield. Putting my hands over my ears, in a futile attempt to shut out the noise, a wave of nausea washes over me.

The mother and baby below me still need to be separated. The game capture team waves a white bag tied to the end of a stick in front of the female. She runs after it, torn between chasing the bag and staying with her young. She charges up the ramp, but runs back down before going fully through the door. Again, she charges at the white bag, but stops short, always returning to her young. I cannot bear it anymore. I feel trapped like the hippo below. Despite my anguish, I cannot look away. I need to witness this for myself to understand the lengths humans have to go to in order to save animals from the wretchedness of mankind. Finally, the mother runs up the full length of the ramp and through the door, the metal door hitting the ground behind her with a sharp, reverberating thud. The young hippo is completely alone—alone in the dark, surrounded by sounds of slamming doors and constant shouting. He no longer has his mother to comfort him. I am bereft.

At 3.30 a.m., we leave. On the drive back to Moholoholo, as I press myself into the furthest corner of the van, it is impossible for me to process the events over the last eight hours. Daniel knows to give me my space. We drive back in silence, exhausted. Some of my fellow volunteers have been crying. I look away, not wishing for them to see that I have noticed. It is 4.30 a.m. when I climb into bed. There is just over an hour to sleep.

My alarm wakes me at 5.45 a.m. for aviary duty. On my way back, I cross paths with one of the game rangers who enquires if I enjoyed the hippo capture. When I tell him that I felt the experience was distressing for the hippos as much as it was for me, he is shocked at my response. He explains that the alternative—culling or living in the wild—would be infinitely worse. While that might be the case, the entire experience for me was harrowing nevertheless. The game ranger informs me that he is under the impression that other volunteers enjoyed the experience. He does not understand my concern, and tells me that I must be the only one who feels this way. Hearing raised voices, a few other game rangers gather around as I try to put my point across, but they say nothing. My attempts to explain my feelings are becoming futile. Not wishing for this heated discussion to escalate even further, I walk away. My anthropomorphism is entirely discouraged, which perplexes me given that animals at Moholoholo have names, and a great deal of effort is spent socialising them. I am disheartened, deflated and utterly disappointed. Here, of all places, I thought I would have been understood. Conservation is nuanced, complex and multi-layered. Sometimes conservation is unpleasant and difficult decisions have to be made, decisions that Moholoholo need to make every day. However, dismissing that animals feel distress, especially under these circumstances, is hard for me to accept.

On my final day at Moholoholo, my trepidation at what lies ahead and the sadness of leaving a place I have grown to love over the past four weeks, follow me in equal measures. Now at another reserve, Tiffany, the grey duiker, is not there to greet me this time. On the way back from my final task of the day, I drink in my surroundings one last time. The Mariepskop Mountains are free of low-hanging clouds, Dela is running away from Darren in an act of growing independence, visitors mill around and volunteers move in and out of the enclosures eagerly completing their tasks. The African fish eagle is squawking, the wild dogs are squabbling over meat put into their enclosure a few minutes earlier, and animals are in their enclosures or roaming free.

After four weeks at Moholoholo, I am ready for something new. While there is no question that staff are dedicated and the work carried out at Moholoholo is crucial, more often than not, it was difficult for me to reconcile the contentious issues of wildlife education, tourism and captivity inextricably linked in a labyrinth of unpredictability. Sometimes it was too hard for me to see so many animals in captivity as a result of man's wrongdoing. Unfortunately, the rehabilitation of wild animals is not always possible, especially for wildlife orphaned far too early. Such needless suffering, animals taken away from their mothers far too young to become "species ambassadors", birds supposed to live in the skies confined to a life contained within fences, and predators incapable of living in wide-open spaces. Moholoholo is, however, a vital part of an enormous web made up of those trying to undo the destruction of wildlife.

After I say goodbye to the lions, Tilo and Duma, whose growls prompted a discussion each morning on the way to breakfast about what they might be saying, I bid farewell to the servals, Scruffball and Emma, and May, the beautiful caracal, an African wild cat with tufted ears and a caramel coat. There are goodbyes too, to the orphaned owls and even to the grumpy lioness who granted me an unforgettable adrenaline-induced experience.

Too rambunctious now for the volunteers and in need of more space, Bullet is now in a larger enclosure. Only staff are allowed to handle him, so I will not be able to stroke him one last time. I feel a strong need to look into his eyes, those amber orbs of immense beauty that stir feelings in me that I cannot yet describe. He ignores my calls to him, more interested in Dela roaming freely beyond his reach.

My last stop is, of course, to Big Boy and Ditch and to Chui close by. They will never know how much their nocturnal grunts and roars of glorious complexity comforted me in the darkness while waiting for sleep to come. Big Boy will never know that his mighty roars created chinks in the armour that cloaks me. Leaning against the fence, the pattern leaves a mark on my forehead. An inaudible "thank you" escapes from my lips, and from my heart.

On the morning of my departure the next day, I don a pair of black shorts and a grey tank top, the paleness of my legs contrasting with my arms now turning golden brown. Shedding the long trousers and sleeved t-shirt feels as if my world is a little lighter, bringing me one tiny step closer to freeing myself from the chains that bind me. The transfer van will take me to Tuli Wilderness in Eastern Botswana, not to Phinda Private Game Reserve with Jenny as planned. Although her good looks often made her the centre of attention, her critical and unkind remarks left behind a wake of discontent, but not before she subjected me to her uncalled-for criticism. She made fun of my fear of the dark, telling me to "get over it", becoming irritated and impatient when I asked her to wait for me so that we could walk the unlit paths to the clinic together to do our evening rounds at 9 p.m.

The knowledge that she would be travelling with me made me increasingly concerned. Phinda only accommodates a few volunteers at one time. Therefore, a positive dynamic among all volunteers would be even more crucial. Living in such close proximity day and night, there would be no room for negativity and toxicity. Having witnessed her behaviour and heard the unkind words she threw out to anyone who displeased her, I refused to spend the next leg of my journey with her. Martin, the *African Conservation Experience* representative who met us at the airport, listened to my concerns and fully understood, having already heard about Jenny's behaviour from several staff members. We decided that I would go to Tuli Wilderness now, instead of in my third month. Now that I had cut up dead chicks, fed moths to dormice and faced raptors, I figured there was nothing a remote place could throw at me that I could not handle. As the minivan spirits me away, Daniel takes my hand. He had long since decided to spend the remainder of his time in Africa with me.

Two travel sickness pills and three hours later, we arrive at the border crossing at Pont Drift. From here, a cable car will carry us out of South Africa, over the muddy, crocodile-infested waters of the Limpopo River, and into Botswana. Had I arrived between June and November, it would have been possible to simply drive across the dry sandy riverbed. Heeding instructions not to hold onto the door of the oversized birdcage in case it opens mid-crossing, I grasp the side instead. Shuddering at first, the metal cage clangs as we clear the tree line and then swings us slowly and steadily across. I imagine these cables that have safely and successfully carried thousands of people will break this one and only time, plunging us to a certain fate. I am a little scared of heights, but I cast these thoughts aside and immerse myself in the beauty of the reflections in the water made by the dense trees and foliage along the opposite bank. The crossing lasts only a few minutes, by which time my unease has subsided and replaced with the excitement of such unexpected transportation.

A lack of foresight to bring food for the journey leaves me ravenous by mid-afternoon. My heart sinks when Bethuel, our driver for the next part of the journey, tells us that it is yet another two-hour drive to the Mohave Bush Camp. The car, clearly older than me, makes its bumpy journey over rocks and pebbles. Holding onto the handle above the window prevents me from slamming my head into the ceiling. We stop to admire two elephants. Absorbed in their beauty and the sheer splendour of the scenery around me, a sudden deafening trumpet of a third behind the car startles me. My jump and loud expletive make Bethuel laugh. The young elephant shakes his head. What will happen if he charges the car? Glancing over to Bethuel, he does not seem bothered at all. I do not know whether to be concerned or comforted by his nonchalance.

We set off again until we run out of road. Tall grasses brush the underside of the car and we follow the path of flattened foliage made by other vehicles. Rolling down the window and extending my arms to film the journey with my point-and-shoot, branches of an overhanging tree smack my arm. The stinging pain is annoying, but I am grateful for not losing my camera.

We stop briefly at Motlhabaneng to drop off a package. This small village, with a population of just a couple of thousand, lies on the north bank of the Motloutse River, near the borders of South Africa and Zimbabwe and on the southwestern boundary of the Northern Tuli Game Reserve. To me, we are in the middle of nowhere, so I am surprised to see a village here. Clusters of rondavel, traditional round, thatched-roof huts, line the village's muddy and dusty paths. Barefoot children playing outside a school drop their ball and wave as we pass. Some run behind us, laughing as they try to catch up. It is an entirely different world here, foreign and filled with hardships that I have never had to endure. I feel like an ignorant intruder.

By late afternoon, we arrive at the unfenced Mohave Bush Camp on the banks of the Mohave River. Daniel and I settle in while we wait for the other volunteers to return. Three mopane-pole huts with thatched roofs, each one raised on a stone floor and arranged in a gentle semicircle, mark one end of the small camping area. Our hut on the right has two single beds and a wooden table. In contrast to the relative luxury of Moholoholo, there is nowhere to store my clothes. I place my hands on my hips and let out a huff of exasperation. Daniel pulls me close, my irritation now dissipating through the gentle caresses of my hair. "Improvise," he says. A few nails driven into the wood provide a perfect place to hang my brown leather bush hat, bought on a game drive to Kruger National Park. While my rucksack is designed for easy access, it is now close to bursting at the seams from the acquisition of clothes one size smaller. Opening it needs to be kept to a minimum.

Placing only the most essential items needed for the next few days in my small rucksack satisfies my need for order. The sound of an approaching vehicle signals the return of the other volunteers. Against a blazing setting sun, six tanned, long-legged girls peer down at us from a Land Rover, inspecting their new guests.

The fire pit is situated just a stone's throw from the huts, the glow from its flames lighting up the otherwise dark night and the faces of my new companions. Lost in deep conversation and eating heartedly from my chipped tin plate, a camel spider scuttles in front of me. With rapid-fire agility, my feet find the safety of the metal bar under my beige camp chair. I will get used to them, I am told. As we swap stories of our African adventures with surprising intimacy, I have the sudden acute awareness that I am in fact sitting in the African wilderness. My initial concerns of such remoteness are long since forgotten.

While curiously comforted that all manner of wild and dangerous animals pass by the camp with regular frequency, the darkness still causes me the most concern. Even though sleep beckons, nature calls. The open-air toilets are a short walk behind the huts. Other than the gas-lit lamps under the thatched roof of the kitchen, the rest of the camp is in complete darkness. Thirty paces might as well be thirty miles. I decide to wait until morning, forgetting that we are going on a game drive and a hike to Eagle Rock before sunrise. When my alarm clock wakes me from a deep sleep at 4.30 a.m., the call of nature is stronger than my fear of the dark. Rather than ask Daniel to accompany me, I choose the route of defiant independence, remonstrating myself for my silliness. Pushing back the mosquito net, I check the ground for spiders with my headlamp. Satisfied, I get out of bed, grab my shoes and walk along the sandy path leading from the huts. My heart pounds in my ears. Worried that I might have left this toilet trip too late, a mouse in the toilet bowl delays me even further. I do not relish the thought of him tickling my skin as he scampers below. Several attempts to free him using the toilet brush fail and he scuttles under the rim. Out of options, I do the unthinkable. I flush. I could have used the adjacent toilet but I am barely holding my nerve. Trying not to think about the mouse, I walk back briskly to join the others. A sigh of relief escapes my lips. I survived.

By 5 a.m., I am wolfing down an apple and yoghurt that Daniel has grabbed for me from the kitchen. I climb into the Land Rover—affectionately known as "the Landy"—to join the other six girls. We space ourselves out. Daniel beside me, I sit at the back on the third banquette, although I soon discover that this is the worst place to be if you have a propensity for motion sickness. Carmen, a deeply bronzed, pint-sized German with an astonishing command of English climbs onto the tracker seat affixed to the bonnet. In such a precarious position, how does she not fall out? I wonder if I will get the opportunity to sit there. Will I be brave enough? Far too early for chat, Stuart, the owner-manager of Tuli Wilderness, drives us out into the darkness, each one of us occupied by our own thoughts. Reflecting on the incident with the mouse and my fear of the dark, I make the spontaneous decision to force myself to walk to the toilets each evening while everyone is at dinner. Perhaps the continuous exposure to my phobia will eventually make me realise that there is indeed nothing to fear.

As night retreats and dawn emerges, Carmen switches off the spotlight. I remain mostly silent, enraptured by the vast vistas of mopane savannah and crisp horizons. Comprising 800,000 hectares, the Tuli Block is a narrow fringe of land at Botswana's eastern border, wedged between Zimbabwe in the north and east and South Africa in the south. It is known for its geographical features, including Solomon's Wall—an area of sheer basalt cliffs reaching thirty metres in height, which once formed a natural dam across the Motloutse River and the Tswapong and Lepokole Hills. The Tuli Block is quite different from anywhere else in Botswana and is called the Hardveld because of the rocky outcrops and the abundance of stones and pebbles. Gigantic Mashatu trees, enormous evergreens with a dense, spreading canopy and drooping branchlets grow out of nutrient-rich termite mounds, and the yellow-barked fever trees grow along the riverbanks. Gaunt sesame trees take root in rocky outcrops, and characteristic baobab trees are ubiquitous amongst the rock koppies. Sandstone hills and rock formations with a system of riverbeds, riverine forests, grasslands and marshes dominate the reserve.

The absence of human habitation is remarkable and it is a relief to know that such large expanses of unspoilt land still exist. Living in concert with animals is a way of life relatively unheard of in the modern world. Villages, power lines or any manmade structure mean intrusion and destruction of animal life and habitat. I often wonder if I am the only person who, when looking out of an aeroplane window, is saddened by the view below—the buildings and lights as far as the eye can see, for more miles than one can possibly comprehend. I wonder too, what these lands might have looked like before man saw fit to wield incalculable carnage. Most would call it progress, but I call it a path to man's own demise; the obliteration of all that was once beautiful in favour of pollution, greed, and dominion over everything that is not human.

A cry from Carmen interrupts my reverie. As we gather around the barely visible marking in the red sand, friendly competition ensues as to who can correctly identify the animal to which it belongs. I cannot even hazard a wild guess. Others try but are invariably wrong. Stuart tells us it is an eland track. Ox-like in appearance, with a thick neck and heavy dewlap, a fold of loose skin hanging from the neck, I had never heard of this spiral-horned antelope before. Each time we stop to examine a track, my desire to be the first to guess correctly and my wish to sit on the tracker's seat grow stronger. However, if this pride of place is to be granted, I will need to pass a test, which is scheduled a week from now.

We drive for several hours, noting the exact location of elephants, impala, zebra, giraffe and other prey animals to determine migration routes and population densities. Upon seeing an elephant, Anne asks me for the coordinates of its location. The simple map in my hands shows the names of the roads, which are clearly marked. However, all I see around me is a sea of green. Eagle Rock, Great Wall of Tuli, Lonely Hill and Tuli Ridge, geographic monstrosities in the far off distance are landmarks to guide me in this still puzzling process. Russet-red tracks masquerading themselves as "roads" make no sense to me. I ask Anne for help again, trying not to stare at her facial hair. She has been here the longest, just over a week, but I am hesitant to ask her because she often meets my questions with a huff of impatience. The map is confusing, and evidently I am not catching on as quickly as she would like. With her reluctant help, I jot down the coordinates in a little notebook.

A curious dynamic occurs among volunteers, one I have witnessed repeatedly since the beginning of my trip to Africa and one that plays out more prominently here in Tuli with only a handful of volunteers. Those who have been at a project for a longer period of time—though often by only a few days—assume a position of authority and an air of bossiness that quashes any suggestion at doing a task differently. A hierarchy of command appears from an invented rulebook I have never been privy to. Out here in the wilderness was the last place I thought I would encounter this, rather expecting an atmosphere of genuine camaraderie. Although, I have only witnessed this behaviour among the female volunteers.

We stop close to the bank of a dry riverbed. It has a precipitous drop down and I can barely believe we will take this route. As we approach, I wonder how the Landy will not tip over. What about Carmen who is not strapped in? She briefly disappears from view as we descend. Gripping the side, the thrill of my perceived danger is exhilarating. Effortlessly, we make it across and up the steep bank on the other side. The others take it in their stride, having done this countless times before.

We start our climb to Eagle Rock, a craggy hill that marks the eastern tip of the Tuli Block, well in advance of the midday sun. In silence, we walk in single file, stopping only when there is a click of fingers signalling an adder or a colourful rock lizard. The climb is not difficult but I fall several times stepping from one rock to another, miscalculating the effort needed to land surefooted. An hour of hiking leads us to the top and to a 360° view that is beyond compare. As blankets of green and blue meet, I feel as though I am wrapped in a postcard.

Wonderstruck by the immense splendour, this place feels oddly familiar, as though the memories of men over millennia have been imprinted in my consciousness. At this precise moment, all feelings of isolation—those I so often felt in the concrete jungle—are absent. I feel more connected to myself than ever before. Looking over at Stuart who is listening attentively to the beeps coming from the telemetry he is holding above his head, he hopes that the radio-collared lion nearby will cross to our side of the river. Stuart is as tall as he is broad, with shaggy, shoulder-length dirty-blond hair, a beard and an infectious hearty laugh. I ask him if he ever feels isolated having lived here for seven years. Before he responds, I already know the answer. His eyes reveal there is nowhere else he would rather be.

The descent is more challenging, although I am pleased that the tread on my boots is preventing the majority of would-be falls. Back in the Landy, we encounter a herd of elephants. Tasked with counting and recording the number of juveniles—those that fit underneath their mother's stomach, my 8x21 binoculars are wholly inadequate and I am cursing not splurging on a better pair. The elephants in the distance, standing behind bushes and walking past each other, are making it difficult for me to count.

A couple of days after arriving at Tuli ('Dust' in Setswana), Stuart informs us that he is planning to track, dart and collar a leopard called Basel. In the first instance, Basel will need to become accustomed to bait covered in human scent. While we organise ourselves for the day ahead, Stuart leaves to find an impala. On my way to the kitchen, two shots in the distance make me stop dead in my tracks. The first, a warning to scatter the herd, the second to kill an adult male. Killing a juvenile or a pregnant female is out of the question. The sound of the flatbed truck signals his return and we pile in. Expecting to see the dead impala in the back, I am relieved when it is empty. When we find him a few hundred yards away, Stuart deftly uses a handsaw, albeit rather a blunt one, to break the skin so that Basel can pick up the scent more easily. The grating of saw against hide makes me wince. We jump down from the truck to take a closer look at the stunning male impala with magnificent horns. My heart squeezes tightly in my chest, not yet accustomed to such sightings. We drive off with the impala tied to the underside of the truck, dragging along the ground.

We choose a tree only minutes from camp to lay this bait. Its proximity will make checking leopard tracks that much easier. With a shovel and rake, we work to clear the area of grass and smooth out the soil. Ropes tied around the impala hoist him higher and between the V of two large branches. While we ponder what to do about the impala's dangling legs, Daniel offers to climb up the tree. Stuart does not see any reason why not. Daniel spent his childhood climbing the large trees in his own back garden. Lean and athletic, he still climbs trees when visiting his parents' house, refusing to let go of his youth. With permission granted, Daniel shimmies up and slings the impala's legs out of the reach of hyenas. Stuart throws his head back and laughs, slapping Daniel on the back when he descends, congratulating him on an act he has never seen any volunteer do before. Daniel's face colours slightly, uncomfortable with the clapping and cheering we are affording him. As we rake the soil again to make it smooth and free of markings, something lands on my arm. At first, I think it is a drop of rain and continue with the task. Then I feel it again. I look up. It is not rain. It is blood dripping from the impala hanging above me. Cleaning it off with the bottom of my t-shirt, I carry on.

After dark, we drive out to check if Basel's footprints have disturbed the smoothly raked soil. There are no prints, nor are there any the following morning. Later on in the day, we find Basel's tracks a mile or two away but he is now going in the wrong direction, possibly from being chased by hyenas. The following day, we return and contemplate how we will get the animal down. Suddenly everyone holds their nose. Ruth is retching. A quiet girl from the UK, and utterly terrified of elephants, her choice of brightly coloured clothing makes me wonder if she did not receive, or simply ignored clear instructions to bring neutral shades to wear.

The smell does not reach me immediately and I wonder what is causing such consternation. Breathing in deeply, the putrid stench of the impala, now dead for two days, wafts over me uninvited, and my urge to retch is swelling. Shallow breathing through the mouth is the only way to get through this. As we lower the impala, the iron pulley almost lands on one girl's head. Tied to the underside of the truck, the breeze dilutes the whiffs of decaying flesh as we drive. Daniel suddenly tells Stuart to stop since the impala has now come loose and is laying on the ground. Attaching it again, we continue until we find Basel's tracks. Again, we hoist the impala up a tree and clear the ground. With fingers crossed, we leave. Basel has not taken the bait the following day. We bring the impala down and leave him for the hyenas. Capturing this leopard is postponed.

On Sunday, there are no game drives. It is a lazy day without hikes, track lessons or population counts. A melodiousness of squawking just outside my hut wakes me early. These sounds delight me, so unfamiliar, so new to my ears. The only call I can distinguish is that of the go-away-bird or grey lourie whose characteristically loud and nasal "kweh" or "go-way" gives him this name. I make a mental note to seek out the bird books that are plentiful at Mohave later in the day to help me with identifying local birds and their calls. Baboon grunts and elephant trumpets add to the already raucous din. All at once, it is silent. I fall back to sleep.

After breakfast, I wash my clothes in a bucket with soap that is not making light work of getting the muddy stains out. I was spoiled at Moholoholo where local women returned fresh smelling and neatly folded clothes every few days. I enjoyed my laundry room trips, greeting these women with a "hello" or "how are you" in their native Sepedi, one of eleven official languages in South Africa. Each day they would teach me something new. We laughed as the words rolled out so differently than they have probably ever heard before. Greeting them in their own language was a way for me to not only ease my guilt of having local women provide a service to a privileged white girl in a foreign land, but also a way to extend a bridge of commonality between women whose lives were certainly poles apart.

My impatience mounts as I hand wash my clothes. I wonder why I feel this way with all the time in the world, with nothing pressing and nowhere to be. Sitting back down on the sandy ground with the bucket at my feet, the pain eases from being in a hunkered position for too long. It is sometimes hard to let go of the deeply ingrained habits formed from a lifetime of fast-paced living in a world that does not wait. Allowing my impatience to subside, I hang my clothes to dry on a nylon cord tied between two trees.

The afternoon is hot, too hot to sunbathe. Daniel and I retreat to our hut, allowing the soft breeze whispering through the gaps in the mopane poles and green netting to temper the rising heat flowing between us. We turn up the volume on his playlist to disguise our fiery desires. Hours later and both perfectly satiated, he looks over at me. "Come back to Rotterdam with me," he says. He knows there is something deep inside me that is locked away, a place he cannot reach. We talk of a life together, yet again, one that can never be. I lay back with my eyes closed as his suggestion rolls around in my head. On the surface, it is entirely plausible to start a new life with him in the Netherlands with Bandit in tow. My belongings can be shipped to anywhere in the world. There is no reason to stay in Canada.

I quite fancy the idea of Rotterdam—in a land of windmills, wooden shoes, tulips, cheese, canals and cyclists everywhere—but these are romantic notions and the reality is steeped in impossibilities and impracticalities. Heading off into the sunset with Daniel would result in alienation by my family. Marrying outside my faith would mean always being talked about in hushed tones as if I had committed the most unthinkable of crimes. I would have to forgo my cultural upbringing, my dream of bringing up a family in a Jewish home, our children sharing two cultures but never truly belonging to any. It would be selfish of me to ask Daniel to learn and adopt the ways of Judaism, to convert but never be accepted by orthodox communities or by most of my family. Neither do I want to be immersed in a life of other traditions; my own cultural upbringing being far too strong. "We'll overcome the obstacles," he says, as I try to explain, but no explanation really conveys the enormous weight of such a decision. "It can never be," I tell him. His eyes declare that he does not fully understand. My whole life, unlike his, has been lived within these parameters, as natural to me as any set of boundaries. This is my life, a life I have always known.

Snow Patrol's "Set the Fire to the Third Bar" plays through his portable speakers. I listen with heightened attentiveness, having never heard this song before. Caressed by the purring softness of the exquisite duet, the lyrics tingle my skin. Seeing my fascination, Daniel sets the song on repeat. *"I'm miles from where you are; I lay down on the cold ground; And I pray that something picks me up; And sets me down in your warm arms."* Mouthing the chorus, he gazes at me with such a rush of intensity that it sets fire to our own third bar, more fervently than ever before.

Leaving Daniel to sleep, I slip out of the hut and walk barefoot to the showers, enjoying the sensation of the sand pushing through my toes. Mopane poles form the shower stalls, high enough to provide privacy, but low enough to see over and across the Mohave River. Showering outside with birds flitting overhead and all manner of insects for company is strangely liberating, my nakedness seeming in tune with my surroundings rather than incongruent. My gratitude for its warmth now cascading down, washing away the dirt of a land brimming with life, is now magnified. I smile and I think back to my conversation with Lisa, the kind staff member at Moholoholo I confided in after my distress at hearing Big Boy roar. One evening, while we chatted on the porch surrounding the girls' accommodation block, she asked me which project I was going to next. When I told her it was to Tuli Wilderness, she smiled widely, having already heard of its magnificent beauty. I told her I was under the impression that there would not be any hot water given the remote nature of the camp. Not that this worried me unduly, not like spiders or my fear of the dark, but as much as I can forgo most things, a warm shower is one I would rather not.

"Don't worry," Lisa said. "Water is heated by a donkey." My eyes grew wider as I searched her expressionless face. What did she mean—a donkey? Images of a lone, pitiful beast of burden walking in a circle attached to some contraption to heat water turned to images of piles of dead donkeys being thrown onto a fire pit, or could it be some other form of barbarity, unimaginable even in my wildest dreams? Swallowing hard, the blood drained from my face, forming an expression of abject horror. Lisa gently put her hand on my shoulder, her smiles now turning to giggles. "A donkey is a metal drum. An open fire below heats the water in it," she said. Joining her in the hilarity, I exhaled in relief.

Emperor moths hinder my turn to cook in the outdated kitchen that evening. The mopane worm, the large edible caterpillar that these moths develop from, provides a source of protein for millions of people. As one of the world's largest moths, its wingspan of 120 mm makes it more than double the size of the Angels Shades moth, the most common moth in the UK. Wings fawn through shades of green and brown to red, with two black and white bands isolating the eyespots. An orange eyespot is present on each hind wing. Attracted by the flickering blue light, one moth flies into the gas-lit hob and flies out, apparently unscathed, while another lands on a fork and feasts on the food stuck to it. Others land on the countertop. Some are attracted to my headlamp while others fly into my face. After serving everyone a choice of meat or vegetarian spaghetti Bolognese, we sit around the fire pit.

Through chatter and clanging of metal forks against tin bowls, I switch between headlamp settings. The main setting will attract moths, but at least it is possible to see if there is one on my fork before my food reaches my mouth. The red setting does not provide the best light for inspecting my food, but it does not attract insects. Every few minutes, I turn on my lamp. No moths. The next time I flick it on to the red setting I find a large moth feasting on my food, its eyes appearing as pink dots as the light is reflected back. Suddenly, I am not hungry anymore. A few more moths follow suit. I leave them to it.

While everyone is chatting, I turn to Daniel and say, "I'll be back." He knows that this means that he must come looking for me if I have not returned from the bathrooms within ten minutes. He laughs because over the past few days, my jaunts have occurred without any incident but the knowledge that he knows where I will be is enough to take the edge off my unease. Putting down my bowl of half-eaten food, I slip away from the comfort of the fire and into the darkness, the chatter becoming muffled. With my headlamp in hand, I remind myself that I walked this same path the night before and the night before that.

My brain searches for what could befall me. I am not a food source for the leopard or lion that I often hear grunting at this time of night—there is plenty of food for them out in the wilderness beyond, and I am sure they would prefer an impala or zebra anyway. Bumping into an elephant is highly unlikely. There are no villages close by and the only other people on site are Kate who bakes our bread and Chris who lights the donkey, both locals whose hut lies a little further back from the bathrooms. Focusing on the beam of light cast by my headlamp, I put one foot in front of the other, congratulating myself for taking a leap of faith and for facing my fears head on. Leaving my headlamp on the side of the sink, I wash my hands and take a moment to stand in the bathroom to gather myself rather than run hell-for-leather all the way back. Walking back to the fire pit as nonchalantly as I can muster, I sit back down in the chair. Daniel turns to me and says, "You are stronger than you realise."

My alarm rings at 4.30 a.m. Reaching for my headlamp from under my pillow and not fumbling for it on the bedside table, allows me to switch off that irritating noise more quickly. Even though I have been away from my normal life in a world that nourishes my spirit, waking up in the dead of night is still a constant battle. While my anxiety is mostly absent during the day and has been for several weeks now, somehow having to wake up so early makes my anxiety visit me in full force, as if it has been storing up all its energy, just waiting for those moments between sleep and consciousness to unleash its power. For so many years, the power of anxiety has gripped me, feeling it cripple me before my eyes are even open. From there it follows a familiar pattern—a crushing weight on my chest; if I did not know any better, I would think that someone was sitting on top of me, except no one is there. Then comes the adrenaline, creeping from my toes to my head, unstoppable and toxic like an oil slick. I lie motionless, unable to calm the quick, shallow breathing and the pounding of my heart. Since my body is incapacitated, I call upon my analytical brain for help and mentally walk through the day ahead, looking for events that will require me to steel my nerve. There are none. Waves of paralysis tell me that impending doom must lie ahead, but logically I know that to be untrue.

For a few minutes, I lie in bed telling myself that it would not hurt to miss the day's outing, but I know it is a decision I will regret if I hear about the amazing adventures second hand. It is as if Daniel can read my deepest conflicts, my attempts to break free from forces that are at odds within me. He turns to me, gently brushing my unruly curls aside, as if to give my anxiety a clear escape from an unencumbered forehead. "The day won't be the same without you. Don't give in to it. I'll grab your breakfast and packed lunch from the kitchen to give you more time."

With a heavy sigh of resignation and annoyance that my anxiety has followed me all the way out into the African wilderness, I turn on my side and cover my head with the blanket. I hear the door open and close as it brushes along the smooth floor. *Which will you regret more? Going or not going?* I ask myself. Out of nowhere, a wave of determination rushes in to meet my wall of disquiet, forbidding my mind to ruin what will be a day of wonder and excitement. In an act of defiance, I throw off the covers and fling back the mosquito net. Automatically scanning the floor for creepy-crawlies before allowing my feet to touch the ground, I dress hurriedly in the cold morning air and pull my fleece a little closer. Climbing into our seats in the Landy, we are lost in thought, our minds still on our warm beds. Following the spotlight as Carmen slowly moves it from left to right, my anxiety abates.

The sight of wild dogs suddenly sends us into a frenzy. We see two. Hunting has brought this species to near extinction and Stuart is concerned for their fate. He hopes that the two we spot are part of a larger group of five he has seen before.

The day of my tracker's test is fast approaching, so I have been paying close attention to the lessons conducted out in the field. Stuart jumps out of the vehicle and, to my surprise, tells me to join him. He informs me that my test is starting. I look down at the track, one I have never seen before. I am not ready. I have only been learning this for just over a week. The thought of failing, when everyone else has passed, fills me with dread. To make it worse, the others gather around, waiting patiently for my answer. Seeing my unease, Stuart changes tack, reassuring me that it is just practice for the next few days. Unbeknownst to me, he is still keeping score.

Over the course of the day, Stuart repeatedly jumps out of the Landy, my cue to follow him. Circling the track on the ground with a stick, he booms, "Wot's it?" I look down, getting my light right. The shadows cast by ridges in a track show up best if the spoor is kept between the tracker and the sun. Facing into the sun, a loud clock ticks in my head as I frantically search my inner database for the correct answer. I am only just learning the *names* of the animals here, never mind discerning their footprint. Distinguishing between a waterbuck and an eland is far too difficult for me just yet. To make it even more challenging, a track looks different depending on the substrate—a track on sand will look different to one on soil. "Wot's it?" Stuart shouts louder, as if somehow that will unlock the answer pounding against my forehead. I give him an answer. Any answer, I feel, is better than no answer at all. When I am wrong, he throws his head back and shouts, "liar!" I laugh at his response and at his maniacal but kindhearted laughter. Stuart's passion is infectious, and one cannot help but feel elated when a track seems suddenly so obvious. I revel in those moments of small victories. The "mock" testing out in the field continues for the next couple of days. In the evenings, I pore over books on track identification.

One late afternoon back at camp after a full day out in the field, Stuart motions for me to join him by the fire pit. The sandy terrain around the living and eating quarters reveal the squiggly lines made by a rake, a task undertaken by Chris, who smooths out the sand every day. A few more times, Stuart asks, "Wot's it?" My answers come easily and fast. Over the past week, I have watched the birds and animals that flit and scurry around the camp, leaving their telltale presence behind. Each correct answer fills me with pride. Stuart finally tells me that the last few days have not been a mock test at all. Having passed with flying colours, the tracker seat will be mine the following day.

Impala potjie is on the menu that evening. Normally, I am relieved to be tucking into a non-meat option, but I find myself pondering the idea of eating this stew. How can I even be contemplating it? I have not eaten meat for over twenty years. The majority of animals raised for food live out their lives in pain and suffering and endure deaths of unimaginable misery. The impala, however, was free, engaging in its natural behaviours in an environment imprinted on it over millennia. With a shot to his head, its death was instant. No suffering. No pain. I feel like a hypocrite for even contemplating the idea. No one bats an eyelid when I put a small portion on my plate. While I enjoy it, I have no desire to eat it—or any meat—again.

Setting off at 5 a.m. the following morning to watch the sunrise, I climb into the tracker's seat for the first time. The crisp, cool air is refreshing rather than unfavourable. Perched on the bonnet, legs dangling, there is an unparalleled feeling of floating through the air, of weightlessness and of exalting liberation. There is a profound sense of stillness, serenity and an abeyance of time. Moving through space as if parting the air in great tides of splendour, my eyes attune keenly to the landscape and scan the surroundings attentively and skilfully.

Statuesque, regal and alone, a large male kudu standing on the side of a hill captures my attention. I blink several times, initially believing that I am mistaken, unaccustomed to seeing one so close. The fringe under his chin, a chevron of white hair on his forehead and corkscrew horns with two full twists give him an air of kingly eminence. The others still oblivious to his presence, we lock gazes and time suspends. He is unafraid, perhaps curious at his onlooker. Unspoken communication envelops me in a sudden rush of warmth that makes my chest fill with an involuntary inhalation of sweet, dusty air. At last, I shout, "KUDU!" He bolts at the sound of a camera shutter, much to my chagrin.

Out of the vehicle, we hike to the Motloutse River. As tracker, I am carrying the first aid kit, and it is my responsibility to lead everyone back to the safety of the Land Rover. Sapped of energy from the almost midday sun and grass seed scratching my ankles, I am pleased when we finally stop to rest awhile. Leaning back against a tree, cooled by the shade of the leaves dancing in the gentle breeze, elephants pass unaware of our presence. Purposefully and gracefully, they walk in single file, millennia of wisdom leading them towards their destination. I close my eyes, allowing my other senses to be heightened—until I hear the unmistakeable flapping of hundreds of red-billed quelea flying just above in a humming swarm.

On the move again, Stuart announces that we must find our way back to the vehicle without his help. I have a poor sense of direction and I have not been paying attention to our route. The landscape is uniform and hilly and we have even walked through cracks in large rocks. The blood drains from my face. I think back to my childhood when my father used to take my younger brother and me on daylong drives on the Floridian I95 or on walks in our favourite park in Dublin. "How do we get back?" my father would ask. I shrugged my shoulders, which prompted more questions of "Which way is east?" and "Where is the sun?" I felt as if the return to the comfort of our home was resting solely on my shoulders. Invariably, the recital of the thirty-two points of the compass at breakneck speed, learned by rote in my father's Scout days, followed my lack of response, although I never quite knew how this torrent of information would provide me with the answers. Never forgetting that dread of feeling utterly lost, in my adult years I always ensured to make a mental note of landmarks or other signposts that would help me find my way back. Annoyed that I have not been paying attention and unable to offer leadership, I default to Anne, who expertly guides us to our waiting green vehicle.

Every two weeks, Stuart makes a trip to the nearest town of Bobonong, fifty-five kilometres away to buy supplies. I leap at the opportunity to see something different. Daniel and I are in the back of one vehicle, a local villager in the passenger seat beside our driver. I know nothing about this man and woman, but for the hour and a half that it takes to get into town, they do nothing but argue. Like an old married couple, they bicker in a language I cannot identify. Daniel looks across at me, shrugs his shoulders and laughs.

He finds it amusing, but I do not. I wish they would stop their fervent hand gestures and that the driver would keep his eyes on the road rather than hurl what I can only guess is another insult at the woman who is not taking his grievances lying down. Leaning my head outside the car window for air provides no relief from the 40°C heat, nor any escape from the heated conversation. When we finally arrive, my head is pounding from the bumpy ride, the raised voices and the oppressive heat. With a population of 19,000, Bobonong has an air-conditioned internet shop. We go directly there, providing us with welcome relief from the stifling heat. After a short reprieve, Carmen, Daniel and I spend some time in Choppies supermarket, which is a similar size and layout as any Western supermarket, its shelves groaning with the sheer number of items displayed upon them. We push a trolley around the aisles, picking up groceries for the staff and volunteers from a list given to us by Stuart, while he and Anne pick up other items elsewhere.

As I put the bags in the boot of the car outside in the large carpark, some emaciated stray dogs catch my attention. With another twenty minutes before it is time to leave, I go back inside and buy some goat stew at the meat counter. One dog wolfs down the entire stew, nearly taking my hand off in the process. The other dogs get nothing. I buy some more. This time I tell the people behind the counter that the stew is for some stray dogs. Their expressions of bewilderment and disgust are evident. I feed the dogs again, now waiting for me outside the supermarket doors.

Still not enough to go around, I go back again, this

time buying two large tins of dog food with pull rings and some plastic knives to prise out the food. The dogs follow me again, still ravenous. In my rush to get them fed, I cut my hand against the tin and blood drips onto the ground. I ignore it at first, more concerned about the starving dogs, then find a tissue in my backpack to stop the bleeding. I know these pitiful dogs are still hungry, but I have spent all my Pula. One of the dogs is blind in one eye. As I put the empty tins in a bin, I hear "Hey, you! The two-legged dog!" I look around and see an old woman in mismatched dirty clothes sitting on the curb in between parked cars. As I walk towards her, she tells me that all she has to eat is the stick she is holding and that she is hungry. Unceremoniously, I tell her that while she has the option of seeking help, dogs are almost solely dependent on their resilience and on the kindness of others. I feel no pity for her.

When I get back to camp, I am told that feeding stray dogs is pointless and futile, that they should be shot or should die so that they do not breed. I completely disagreed but I had neither the energy nor the inclination to argue with such an ingrained and unmovable line of reasoning. I could not fix the situation, but I could ease their hunger, perhaps giving these dogs the energy for a few hours to find food elsewhere. I was unwilling to do nothing. Small acts of kindness have ripple effects.

Now in my second week at Tuli, Moholoholo was beginning to feel like a lifetime ago. Daniel left a few days ago after one of our early morning drives. He returned to

Rotterdam, back to his normal life. He had only planned six weeks away and now it had come to an end. He had to resume job hunting. In the days leading up to his departure, I found myself increasingly subdued, unable to engage and partake in the animated banter around the fire pit at night or to laugh at the jokes everyone would make about the minutia of the day's events. There was nothing more to say. I could not be a part of his life, nor could he be part of mine. From the first day I met him, I knew it could never be. I resigned myself to being totally immersed in the richness that can be gained from transient relationships. For decades, best friends have been hard to come by. Moving countries made that prized relationship even harder to obtain. Once over the grief of living far away from my childhood best friend, I began to learn the value of meaningful relationships that come and go, being grateful for them while they last and accepting the void they leave behind when it ends.

With bags packed, he hugged everyone goodbye, leaving me until last. All eyes were on us as we embraced; a private moment made so very public. "I'll miss you," I whispered in his ear as he held me tight, just for a few moments more. We parted, and I watched his transfer van disappear into the distance. As I climbed back into the Landy, I was grateful for my dark sunglasses. Questions posed to me for the rest of the day were met with a forced smile and a succinct response.

Standing in the doorway of the hut later that day, my eyes adjusted to the darkness within. It felt larger than when I left it that morning. The space around me felt empty, the world suddenly bigger, the bed oversized rather than beckoning. For the past six weeks, Daniel had been at my side, making my life easier in subtle ways—grabbing my breakfast, holding out a hand when navigating rocky terrain, and carrying my backpack when I needed to squeeze through rocks. But, most of all, he listened with curiosity and intensity, giving me a no-nonsense interpretation of what troubled me, unlocking alternative solutions otherwise unattainable from my thoughts alone. We spent heady, lazy afternoons at Tuli in the privacy of our hut, talking about everything and nothing, out of the burning sun and away from the sometimes-envious glares. I suddenly felt very alone, something I had not felt since landing in South Africa.

In the days that follow, I pay more attention to the beauty of my surroundings at camp in my free time. Settling into my favourite spot overlooking the Mohave River, I enjoy the antics of a group of banded mongoose that venture out onto the dry riverbed in search of beetles and millipedes in the late afternoons. They make me laugh as they bob their heads up and down, exchanging little squeaks and imparting all manner of important information. A rock lizard slowly makes its way past. I imagine my delight at seeing an elephant herd so close to camp but they do not come. Sometimes I sit in front of a tree just outside my hut to watch a yellow-billed hornbill feeding her chicks or the Maeve's starlings cooling themselves in a water bowl. Squirrels scoot up trees and scamper across the sand, leaving tracks that lead me to their whereabouts. I while away a few hours with sunbathing, evening out the tan lines created by hours of driving under the sun. Deeply bronzed in a nearly all-over tan, the one-size-smaller pair of shorts bought a couple of weeks ago are now too loose.

In the nights that follow, my bathroom visits continue without the comfort of knowing that Daniel will search for me before too long has passed. My trips so far have been uneventful. I walk more slowly with each passing evening, allowing myself to listen to the sounds of the night, all the while ensuring to make enough noise to frighten anything away with my footfall. Each return to the fire pit brings me a little closer to freeing myself of my fear.

Only Carmen, Anne and Ruth remain now, so for the weekend, we move to Serolo Safari Camp, mainly to avail of the electricity to power the computer. Located along the shady floodplain of the Limpopo River, it is just 600 metres from the river itself, under the many massive riverine trees, including the magnificent Mashatu and tall Apple-leaf. The large high-end tents for tourists have an ensuite bathroom, two beds with bedding in a bold African print, a side lamp and a porch on three sides. In the evening, we each retreat to our own tent. I slip into bed, immersed in *Tippi of Africa*, the story of a real-life Mowgli, a child born to French parents who spent the first ten years of her life in Namibia befriending and communicating with all manner of wild and dangerous animals, believing they were her brother and sisters.

We chat to each other about plans for the next day, our voices carrying easily in the night air. "What was that?" Ruth suddenly whispers, her voice layered with growing alarm. I put down my book and listen, presuming she is alarmed yet again at the sound of an elephant rumble or trumpet. The mere word *elephant* makes her tremble with fear. We see countless elephants out on our drives and much time is spent allaying her fears. She is leaving Tuli two weeks earlier than planned because her nerves are fraught. I wonder why she chose to come here in the first place but I refrain from asking having already witnessed her defensive response when Stuart asked her the same question. Listening closer still, I know with absolute certainty that it is the roar of a lion. How could I mistake that sound after weeks at Moholoholo hearing Big Boy's roars during the day and often at night? "It's a lion," I tell them. "How do *you* know," Anne asks in that "I know better than you" tone I have come to recognise. "Because I spent four weeks listening to a lion roar," I respond matter-of-factly. "We'll ask Stuart in the morning," Anne says, settling the matter. The others agree that this is the best course of action. Ruth says she is still afraid and Anne and Carmen try to allay her fears for yet another half an hour. I go back to reading.

The soft grunting of a leopard in the distance lulls me to sleep, but crickets and raucous baboons wake me early the next morning. First to stir, I sit back into one of the porch chairs, allowing myself to revel in the solitude and peacefulness beneath the canopy. Four curious vervet monkeys come within feet of the porch and I wish they would come even closer still. All too soon, these small grey, black-faced masters of the trees find something more interesting so off they go, one by one. Not long afterwards, more rustling reveals a couple of adult warthogs. Knowing how dangerous they are, I have no desire for them to come any closer.

Before the others have risen, I sit in the lapa, the thatched-roof gazebo supported by wooden poles, to read and eat my breakfast of fruit and yoghurt. The hum of an approaching vehicle signals Stuart's arrival. The crunch of several zippers opening and closing simultaneously is followed by the soft slapping of three pairs of flip-flops hastily making their way over to Stuart who is now in the nearby kitchen. From where I am seated, I overhear the conversation in tones of disquiet and eagerness to answer their burning question as to what they heard the night before. Upon hearing Stuart's response, I smile and return to my book.

Later in the afternoon, after inputting the collected data into a computer with a cracked screen, we all sit in the lapa taking respite from the sun. Four red-billed hornbills perch themselves only a few metres away. Bobbing their bodies up and down, their squawking makes it impossible to read. In the distance, elephants are tearing down trees but I decide not to tell Ruth, who is listening to her iPod beside me. However, she did not mind when a small spotted genet poked his head into her tent. Having only seen two at Moholoholo I would have liked to have seen this one living freely.

Back at Mohave a few days later, washing my teeth in the dead of night, thoughts of how far I have come over the past few weeks occupy my mind. The darkness that once felt so menacing, feels far less so now. Turning off my headlamp, I place my hands on the white porcelain sink and breathe deeply, allowing myself to feel the cool night air one last time. The soft grunting from a leopard does not alarm me. For several nights now, he has accompanied me on my nightly trips before bed. Slowly and calmly, I walk back to my hut, imagining the beauty of the leopard I will never see, but secretly hoping to catch just a glimpse. My bags are packed, zipped and at the ready. Although I am leaving Tuli in the morning, the wilderness will stay with me forever.

Stuart drives me over the border to the town of Alldays, back to South Africa and leaves me to wait for my transfer in a delightfully small modern café, with a gift shop inside. Mixed emotions jostle for my attention as we say our goodbyes. A part of me wishes to stay at Tuli Wilderness, where memories of Daniel enriched my experiences, where days ebbed and flowed; days that were simple, stripped back, unadorned and unencumbered by material things. I feel fortunate to have experienced a relationship rooted in a mutual love of wildlife, one that flourished in a world so far removed from the one we both know, far removed too from everything I usually take great pains to perfect—the expensive makeup, stylish clothes and the carefully crafted narrative that conceals the truth.

Another part of me craves a new adventure, ready now to shake off fanciful hypotheticals and pangs of disappointment, to free myself of volunteer dynamics and tiptoeing over a minefield of egos. I am done with the competitiveness and one-upmanship that have spoiled these otherwise exhilarating days. Now, I find myself yearning to form strong bonds, to push past this superficiality and the trivial concerns that have become so ingrained in our lives.

With only a handful of volunteers and Daniel by my side, Tuli was initially a welcome refuge from such irksome puerility that I witnessed at Moholoholo. However, in the week that Daniel left, six of us made the two-hour journey to Phikwe, a town of 50,000 people. We went directly to the internet café for a reprieve from the heat and access to the outside world. After an hour absorbed in sending emails to friends and family, I looked up to find myself completely alone. The chairs behind me were suddenly empty. I sat back, scanning my brain for an explanation but I was at a loss. I stood up abruptly, the chair squeaking along the floor as it moved behind me. Throwing my belongings into my bag, I hurled the paper coffee cup into a recently emptied bin, resulting in a thud. Muttering to myself in disbelief, I slung my bag over my shoulder and threw open the door. Blinded by the sunlight, I reached for the sunglasses still resting on my head.

Standing in the doorway, I looked around, the heat forming beads of sweat on my forehead. Even though we were explicitly instructed to stick together, now I found myself alone in a strange town with no means of contacting

Stuart or anyone with whom I had travelled. I was left with no choice but to wander the almost empty streets, frantically scanning for someone—anyone—I recognised. Sticking out like a sore thumb, I ignored the stares and peered into the shops and cafés until I eventually found them in a restaurant, casually ordering lunch as if they had not just walked out and left me. I approached their table, their chatter stopping in an instant when they saw me. All eyes were on me when I asked them why they had left unannounced. Anne's answer was blasé, detached, but calculatingly composed. She told me that I simply must not have heard them leave so engrossed in my internet endeavours.

Sensing that this had been a collective decision, I knew that arguing against this feeble response would only isolate me further. I acquiesced, admitting that it was my fault. In the eyes of the instigator and those who sheepishly followed, I saw their guilt, their recognition of an unkind and undeserved deed. The tentacles of exclusion had reached me even here. Although I searched my mind for reasons why I had been treated so, I failed. For the rest of my stay at Tuli, my mask returned.

At the café in Alldays, I order breakfast, thrilled to be drinking freshly ground coffee from a sparkling white porcelain cup instead of a plastic or tin mug. With a few hours to spare, I am content to be alone with my thoughts, speculating about what the next two weeks will bring. I never expected to be here, heading to a place where horses replace all-terrain vehicles. The news that the Game Ranger course was no longer going ahead initially sent waves of unease hurtling through my veins. Uncharacteristically, I dismissed my disquiet quite promptly, focusing instead on the array of choices put before me. Unshackled from the whirr of doubt and grounded in unswayable intuition, my decision came quickly.

Ordering a second cup of coffee, I move to a table in the adjacent garden, where sweet-smelling plants and multi-coloured pots beckon to be carried away to deliver joy to those who should gaze upon their gaiety. John, the manager at Hanchi Horseback Conservation, strides up to my table and shakes my hand, gripping it a little too hard in his exuberance. Sitting down, he too orders a coffee and our conversation flows freely and easily. He laughs when I tell him of my delight at eating from white china plates and then at my expression when he tells me I will be eating from tin plates again.

After a half-hour drive to Hanchi, Kirsten is the first to welcome me. Tall, blonde and Dutch, our initial conversation is animated, moving quickly past superficiality and delving into what matters to us most. Immediately I know we will be friends long after our days together in South Africa. Without a close bond since Daniel's departure, I welcome this new friendship with open arms. Having recently arrived at Hanchi and planning to stay for one month, she relays that her boyfriend of just five months presented her with a gift before her departure. A small flip chart of handwritten love notes, one for each day of her trip, lays under her pillow to allow her to feel his love from so far away at moments when she needs it most. I am amazed and intrigued at her leaving for what seems to me to be a long time, considering her absence might well be their unmaking, and the time he has taken to make her such a gift to accompany her along her journey. Struck by their mutual trust, I wonder what it is like to feel so secure of someone else's feelings.

When conversations die down, Kirsten shows me to my tent, one of five in a row. With two beds inside and nowhere to store my clothes, the second bed becomes home to my backpack. Reluctant to use mosquito repellent due to its toxicity and repugnant smell, I immediately erect the net. Tiny bloodstains dot the white mesh.

The next morning, my alarm rings at 5.45 a.m. but I have been awake for at least an hour. The yellow-billed hornbills, Natal-francolins, Cape turtle doves and other birds I do not yet recognise have already started their calls. Too noisy to go back to sleep, I dress quickly to avoid the pestiferous mosquitoes that have found their way into my tent despite my best efforts of zipping up all the zippers. Wood and kindling from the surrounding bushes and a healthy dose of paraffin bring my fire to life. My donkey will provide me with hot water upon my return.

After a quick breakfast, Kirsten and I join Alyssa in a Land Rover for the five-minute ride through the bushveld, under an electric blue sky, to the ranch-style stables. Upon opening the creaky wooden gate, Monty, a one-year-old German Shepherd Rottweiler and Millie, a Rhodesian ridgeback, jump at me almost knocking me over. They are rambunctious, energetic, and wanting of attention. Stern reprimands and the ensuing commotion make Monty jump even more. Remembering my instructions when handling Bullet, I tap Monty on the nose and firmly say, "No." Again, he jumps and he receives the same response. A few more taps and finally both dogs are calm by my side. Alyssa asks me if I am a dog whisperer, having never seen Monty behave so quickly around a new person. Secretly wishing I were, I laugh and rebut her ludicrous suggestion. I revere those who have this ethereal gift.

Belly rubs and unadulterated affection ensue with ample licks to my face, but not before I free them of ticks the size of thumbnails, leaving splodges of blood on the pebbly ground as I crush them with my shoe. Freed of this irritation, the dogs follow me to the horses with tails wagging high.

Nine rescued former-racehorses wait patiently in their stalls, except for Gunsten who has escaped from his yet again. The horses, each one with their own personality that will become apparent as the days pass, poke their head through the large window and whinny in anticipation of fresh feed. After stuffing as much hay as possible into a net, I set about tying it to the ceiling beams overhead. A nearby chair helps me climb onto the narrow windowsill, several feet from the ground. Holding the side of the concrete window frame, I crouch slightly to accommodate the low ceiling. I stand there for a few moments, precariously balanced and wondering how I will hang the nets. I will need both hands to tie the rope around the beams, but my left hand is gripping the side of the window to prevent me from falling. Surely, there has to be an easier way to do this. Looking around at the other volunteers, some have already hung a couple of hay nets in the time it has taken me just to get onto the windowsill. Cotton nuzzles me in her impatience, threatening to push me off balance. I tell her that she must wait and that I simply cannot fall or fail at this task. Positioning myself the best I can, I throw the rope over the beam and tie it quickly. I grab the side of the window and lower myself, relieved to have the chair to help me get down. My thigh muscles scream at me as I climb and balance on another three windowsills. General, the 23-year-old gentle giant, is the only one who waits until I have hung the net before he tucks in. Abused by his former owner, he has a large scar running the length of his back, so I speak to him with extra softness.

While the horses eat, it takes us two hours to muck out the stables filling eight wheelbarrows. Stopping for a few moments to allow the strain of such exertion to abate, the purple-hued dung beetles fascinate me as they move backwards, rolling balls of dung in a straight line despite the obstacles in their way. There is a strange pleasure that comes from freeing those from a wheelbarrow that might otherwise be crushed from the weight of additional manure. Dozens of butterflies suck moisture out of the freshly produced dung in perfect symbiosis. How far removed we are from such reciprocity. Waste is solely a human-driven phenomenon.

The first riding lesson of my life is with Cotton. Diminutive beside her and with no prior experience with horses, I am nervous, gingerly brushing her chestnut brown coat. Cotton lowers her head and as she turns to look at me, all apprehension melts away. Instinctively I know that she trusts this complete stranger and an equine husbandry novice in charge of making her mane shine and her coat glossy. Cotton is still, besides the occasional movement of her head and swish of her tail, her neck silky soft and velvety against my cheek that unconsciously finds itself there. Whispers of nonsensical ramblings that make perfect sense to me tumble from my lips. In response, Cotton tickles my hair with her lips, reminding me how much I have missed physical proximity to animals.

Cotton is neither concerned nor embarrassed when she passes gas, a consequence of lifting her tail to groom these long coarse strands. Then, Alyssa shows me how to clean the hooves, expertly lifting Cotton's right leg and freeing the V of debris. Alyssa then hands me the hoof pick. I glide my left hand down Cotton's front left leg, tugging gently to encourage her, but she does not lift her leg. I tug some more. Still Cotton does not cooperate. I ponder what to do. I find Alyssa, now in the tack room. She joins me again beside Cotton and suggests that I bend forward and lean against Cotton's body, facing away from her head. Still not entirely comfortable around horses and hesitant to ask a strong-willed horse to do something against her wishes, I fight my reaction to protest. I do as instructed. Bending forward, I reach down and glide my hands down her left leg. I tug gently and Cotton yields to my request. Moving quickly, I clean out her hoof, taking advantage of her compliance before she changes her mind. My luck runs out with her hind hooves. Alyssa obliges me. Satisfied with my grooming, Alyssa helps me with the saddle and bridle by affixing the straps and buckles at a speed that only comes from years of equine expertise. From Finland, she has been riding since the age of six.

Now in the grassy paddock, I slide my left foot into the left stirrup and hold onto the pommel with my left hand and the cantle with my right. I hop three times. The last hop propels me onto the shiny brown saddle in a movement resembling one practised in the art of mounting a horse, or so Alyssa tells me. Apprehension quickly replaces my initial elation of getting onto the saddle so deftly. I feel too high up, insecure and unprotected, but Alyssa urges me to relax, to allow my hips to move in tandem with Cotton's movements. Instead of concentrating on my pounding heart, I focus on this unfamiliar motion. A swell of colliding emotion takes me unawares. A lump in my throat is forming and tears are threatening to fall. I hear my inner voice screaming. *Not here. Not now!* Fixating on a spot on a distant tree helps me pay attention and allows me to compose myself. There is no time now to figure out why being on top of a horse unhinges emotions I thought were safely guarded. The hour-long session is over all too soon. My dismount is inelegant and unimpressive.

For three days, I groom Cotton and practice walking around the paddock. By now, I am anxious to leave its confines to ride out in the bush, but I must master the basics. On the fourth day, my riding lessons continue, but not with Cotton who is strong-willed and eager to ride fast. Instead, I am paired with Farwell, who is also chestnut brown with black stockings. He is happily munching on hay with Kalahari, a dark-brown horse with a glorious golden mane, Max, the leader, and Gunsten. Farwell is none too pleased when I take him away to be groomed. The curry comb removes most of the dirt caked into his coat from him rolling in the mud. I brush him with purpose, anxious to see his coat shine. I talk to him, this time not caring if anyone is listening. I ask him to be gentle with me since I am very new to riding. He lets me clean his front hooves but not those of his hind legs. Unwilling to force him to do something he does not want, Alyssa assists me.

With the numnah correctly placed at the withers and the saddle buckled and strapped, I set about putting on the bridle. Putting my hand around his face, I hold the bridle with my right hand, offering the bit with my left. Invariably, Farwell keeps moving his head, making this task rather challenging. I wish he did not have to wear this infernal contraption.

Hopping three times, I am up. Stiff from riding, shovelling and wheelbarrowing, I feel every muscle in my body. Although I squeeze my legs against Farwell, he does not budge. Again, I squeeze and say, "Come on, Farwell". Still he does not move. I start to wonder if it is my command. Alyssa laughs. Evidently, I have been watching too many westerns because 'whoohoo" and "yee-haa" clearly do not work. At Alyssa's suggestion, I make a clicking sound as

I squeeze my thighs against him. Farwell complies. While the other volunteers prepare their horses, I walk in circles around the paddock. My ride out into the bush is only minutes away.

First in line is Alyssa on Zoro, a large dappled-grey horse who, despite his name, is scared of everything. Rachel on Kalahari rides behind. Maggie on Empire rides behind me. Pretending to be perfectly at ease quells my growing excitement and trepidation. A few minutes pass, but nothing untoward happens, giving me much-needed encouragement. However, when Farwell suddenly bends his head to eat the grass below, it pulls me forward almost causing me to fall off. I tell Farwell not to give me a fright like that again, but he does. For the first half an hour, a battle of wills ensues. Soon he realises that he must only eat grass when we stop.

The free-roaming roan antelope in the 8500-hectare reserve are nonplussed when they see us. The horses do not seem to notice them until one roan suddenly bolts, spooking Kalahari. Farwell jumps to the side as well, throwing me off balance. Grabbing the saddle to stop myself from falling, it takes me several minutes to calm myself. After an hour out in the bush, I am relieved when my feet touch the ground back at the stables.

Dinner that evening, set outside on a large wooden picnic table, is a feast. We pile our plates with salads, butternut and gem squash, French toast, and vetkoek, a traditional Afrikaner fried dough bread filled with honey, although I opt out of the babotie, a South African dish of minced meat baked with an egg-based topping. Stories of our animal encounters, our lives and plans for the next few days swirl over our heads. Attracted to the gas lamps, bees, moths, praying mantises and other insects carpet the table in a blanket of wings and legs.

Tired from my exhilarating excursion in the bush, I retire earlier than the others. Although my tent is a good seventy paces from the dining area, I am not afraid to walk along this unlit path as long as I have my headlamp. Peering into the darkness up ahead and pleased with myself that the darkness no longer grips me, I notice a pair of eyes reflecting back at me. Impala, I tell myself, but why would one be so close? I keep moving forward, albeit a bit more slowly as I try to figure out what animal it is. The eyes, however, are not moving. To me this is strange. Is it a leopard, laying deathly still, waiting to pounce? Despite my nervousness, I continue walking, my eyes fixed on the shining dots in the distance. Just as I reach my tent, I stop and laugh—half in relief and half at my ridiculousness. They are not the eyes of a leopard in waiting, but the reflective material on the back of my runners that I had left on a small table.

Each afternoon, we head out into the bush, going farther each day. Puffy white clouds dot the blue sky above, and verdant vegetation of different shapes and sizes flank the grassy trail. The clicking of hooves and the swishing sound of horses moving through the long grasses lull me. Birds fly from this tree to that and a raptor circles above. No longer frightened at being up so high, I sometimes forget I am on horseback. Riding out in the bush brings me a peace that

I never thought possible, each swaying movement bathing me deeper in a protective swathe of serenity. Farwell's head moves up and down as he walks, his brown coat glistening in the sun, changing colour with the shifting of light. My body rocks, perfectly aligned with his movements. I feel completely free as if I can accomplish anything. My confidence now, knows no bounds.

The following day, I hang six hay nets with agility and speed, barely needing the chair to aide my ascent onto the narrow windowsills. Leaner and stronger now after seven weeks of almost constant activity, I wonder how I would have fared had this been the first project of my trip.

In the afternoon, I join the predator monitoring group to check on Rebecca, a collared cheetah. Spotting her sitting under a tree, I think of Bullet and wonder if he will ever taste the freedom he so richly deserves. Leaving her in peace, we drive some more. A couple of hundred vultures sitting on numerous trees indicate that there must be a fresh kill nearby. We drive on to find a half-eaten wildebeest. The stench is nauseating, leaving me to fight the retching that has involuntarily engulfed my body. Eaten down to the bone, its head is still intact. I take pictures, not knowing why this grotesque sight is so fascinating.

On the way back to camp, we pass a cluster of houses and I enquire about the painfully thin dogs in the backyard. Although they were rescued and slowly putting on weight, there are plans to shoot them. Formerly used by poachers who deliberately kept them starving, their instinct to kill animals is far too strong. Over the days that follow, this information weighs heavily on my mind. I curse my curiosity that so often leads to knowledge that is too much for me to bear.

The following morning, I am awake hours before it is time to get up. Barely light, I pull on a fleece, unzip the door of my tent, and slip into my flip-flops. Still half asleep, I almost walk into a golden orb spider suspended in an intricate web—one strong enough to trap small birds—spun diagonally across the bathroom. I slowly back out, scarcely believing that I sidestepped a dreadful encounter. Too early to wake anyone, I decide the bushes will have to do.

At the stables now, I have forgotten about my untimely encounter with the golden orb. After a good brush down, interspersed with kisses and hugs, I lead Cotton to the training paddock. Expertly settling into the saddle, as if I have been doing this for months, I spend a few minutes walking in advance of learning to trot. I am nervous about riding faster and only slightly comforted that Alyssa can bring my horse to a stop in an instant.

My first few attempts at trotting are unsuccessful, feeling off balance and certain I will fall off. Gathering myself and unwilling to be defeated, I eventually trot the full length of the paddock and soon ten seconds becomes thirty and then long enough to feel its unique rhythm. The feeling of flying through the air cascades over me in a tidal wave of unfamiliar sensations, and a yearning to cling on to this upsurge of unadulterated joy, this swell of freedom, penetrates every fibre of my being. I trot around the paddock as though suddenly intoxicated.

My trotting lessons end and I dismount feeling dizzy and euphoric, but it is late afternoon and there is no time to linger. Farwell, Zoro and Bikini have been in a fenced-off portion of the cheetah camp munching on grasses since early morning and they must be back in the stables before dark. Fetching our saddles and bridles from the tack room, we walk for ten minutes along the dusty trails and out into the bush. How utterly natural it feels to be walking through the bush to pick up my horse, how remarkable but yet as accepted as breathing. The saddle is heavy, my arms folded underneath to support its weight. Falling a little way behind Alyssa and Rachel, my legs are not carrying me as fast as I would like. The setting sun casts a heavenly glow over my two companions a short distance ahead. The air is still warm and sounds of nature fill the air. At this very moment, a feeling of immense peace envelops me, taking me yet again by complete surprise. Suddenly, I feel connected to the environment around me as if now I can see the once invisible webs that connect everything. It is as if I have spent my entire life living in the fringes, an onlooker to the connectivity but never feeling it. But, now I feel it, and so acutely as though I can touch the "present", the "now" obliterating any concern over the staggering mountain of issues facing me post-Africa. My reverie of staying here forever, riding horses through the bush seems entirely plausible.

Having heard us approaching, our horses are already waiting for us at the gates. It does not take me long to settle comfortably on Farwell. In Bikini's excitement to return to camp, she starts trotting. Farwell follows her lead. 'No," I cry out, pulling on the reins. I tell Farwell he is not allowed to trot, having only practiced for one hour on a much smaller horse. Somehow, he understands and slows to a gentle walk. He does not even try to eat the grass, not even once. Putting him in his stable for the evening, I stay with him a little longer in my reluctance to leave. Later, cocooned in my mosquito net, with only my thoughts for company, my mind wanders to the drive to the White Dam the next day.

Franki, a fearless, ninety-pound, nineteen-year-old German, drives me out to the Plains. We pass through terrain I have come to adore, atop of a horse I have come to love even more. The Blouberg Mountains throw their jagged shape in the distance, framing my view in a tranquil embrace. Set among the terrain of sparsely covered trees and low-lying yellow grass is a pool of shimmering clear blue water, flanked by banks of desiccated white mud. I get out of the vehicle slowly, barely believing that such a place exists. Franki is talking to me but her words are nonsensical muffles. How could there be a place more beautiful than the expanse of the Tuli wilderness? This is the White Dam I have heard so much about.

Sitting on the bank, Franki nonchalantly tells me she canters here with Empire. I turn to look at her in both amazement and in disappointment. To canter to such a place must bring such rapture, a feeling I dare not even imagine. Not only is my trotting not of sufficient standard to ride out this far, but also my transfer to Phinda is only a few days away. I remove my shoes and allow the cool water to lap at my feet, hoping that it will shake the sudden heaviness that has enveloped me unannounced. As I gaze off into the distance, Alyssa and Rachel arrive on horseback. I watch as they dismount and remove the saddles, leaving them on the white caked mud. They mount again. Bikini paws the water, enjoying the coolness reaching her belly. I can only but watch from the other side of the bank, imagining how freeing it must be to ride bareback through such pristine water in a place that resembles the closest to paradise I have ever seen. Cursing that I do not know how to trot and cannot partake in this glorious experience, I decide not to leave until I too have ridden bareback here in the place of shimmering blueness. Back at the stables, Alyssa promises to take me here on Farwell on my last day, once I have learned to trot. My spirits immediately brighten, and I postpone my departure for one more week.

For the next five days, my trotting lessons continue. Despite my exhilaration and amazing progress the first day, my double bouncing is causing me great concern. I cannot go to the dam, which is an hour's ride away, if I cannot trot correctly. My frustration mounts, unsure why trotting is not coming as easily as I had hoped. The date of my transfer to Phinda is one day earlier than expected, so now there is no choice but to go to the White Dam the next morning.

Rising at 5 a.m., my excitement is barely controllable. We must leave the stables at 7.30 a.m. if I am to make it to the dam and back in time for my transfer. The air is cooler than normal and dark clouds in the distance are not encouraging. I groom Farwell all the while talking to him, cooing softly. I know he understands me and he nuzzles me in response. Leaning against his body, I clean his hooves without any resistance. Attaching his saddle and bridle comes more naturally and efficiently this particular morning. While waiting for Alyssa and Zoro, I lead Farwell out to the courtyard. The sound of the metal stirrups as they slide down the leather and slap as they reach the bottom makes my body tingle with excitement.

The clicking of hooves on pavement turns to soft footfalls. It is warmer now but the clouds in the distance are troubling. If it rains, we must turn back. We ride on even though Farwell is coughing. Alyssa signals to Zoro to trot. I do the same, heels down and thighs squeezed, no longer double bouncing. There is still another half an hour of trotting to go before we make it to the place of shimmering waters. Spots of rain fall upon Farwell's glistening coat but I trot on, unwilling to be deterred. The sporadic raindrops become more frequent as a thunderstorm threatens in the distance. Alyssa stops and signals that we cannot go any further. We must turn back before the storm reaches us. Alas, my dream of floating bareback is not to be.

Farwell carries me back to the stables where I say goodbye to the horses who intrigued me every day with their antics. Leaving Farwell until last, I stand slightly to his side to accommodate his range of vision. His liquid black eyes now do not show the normal hint of mischievousness. Instead, they bore into my soul and signal his recognition that I must leave. He bids me goodbye, wrapping my heart in a blanket of eternal devotion.

Alyssa drives me to Alldays one last time. Kirsten joins me, taking advantage of the weekly town trip. At the café, we indulge ourselves in a cappuccino and laugh at how simple our pleasures have become. All too soon, the time comes for me to leave. Tears threaten to rise to the surface. Kirsten and I have become great friends, having shared so many stories, endlessly ruminating on our days' experiences, finding amusement in the tiniest of details. She had become a friend with whom I could share life's exploits without judgment or misunderstanding. I feel lucky to have found such a rare and elusive bond at Hanchi.

At the departure gate at Johannesburg Airport, the din grates on my nerves. Choosing a ninety-minute plane journey to Richard's Bay over a nine-hour drive is little comfort to me now. Continuous blaring flight announcements, kids shouting while their parents let them "be children", the sniffing of too many people with colds, and the harsh glare of fluorescent lights are an assault on my senses. Scowling and willing for everyone to be gone, I wish to be gone—away from this manmade world of straight lines and sharp edges. My fingernails leave moon-shaped indents on my palms.

The aeroplane hum, the stale cabin air and sandwiched between two men manspreading only adds to my rising frustration. However, an article in the on-board travel magazine piques my interest. The author depicts the thrill of leopard tracking in the Sabi Sands Game Reserve so accurately through his rich, descriptive prose that it allows me to escape through an invisible porthole into a world of endless delight for a blissful ten minutes. Tearing out the article in my daydreamy state, I wonder if I might one day bestow the same gift onto others.

My transfer to Phinda ('the Return' in Zulu) takes two hours. Finally turning off the monotonous highway onto a dirt road, all tension from the past twenty-four hours escapes my body in one long audible sigh. Music is playing from the rustic farmhouse when the van pulls up in front. Thrilled to see Courtney from Moholoholo, which now seems like a lifetime ago, we hug tightly, knowing that each one of us is tougher than when we last met and there are stories to be told and secrets to be kept. The nights will hear those stories and be a keeper of those secrets. Rachel is also here, arrived from Hanchi a week earlier. She is the life and soul of any group, with a dry sense of humour and the ability to drink anyone under the table. The other house residents are students and researchers. A lightness and joy fills the house.

But there is no time to linger and unpack with careful precision. J.P., unassumingly handsome, with ruffled hair and sun-kissed skin, tells us we need to leave to search for one of the collared lions. I jump into the front seat of the Landy, reserved for newly arrived volunteers. The noisy green machine is comforting, familiar, known. I have been in so many game drive vehicles, I wonder how I will adjust to any other—especially one with a roof! We drive along dirt tracks that wind through the rare sand forest, so many trees I have never seen or heard of before. J.P. satisfies my growing need to know the names of the most common trees and plants. Only in his early twenties, he knows the scientific and common names of hundreds of local fauna and flora. I am mesmerised and in awe at someone so young who holds such an encyclopaedic knowledge. Over the noise of the engine, he tells me that he does not read any book that cannot teach him something useful. I think back to all the trivial publications I have read over the years and I am struck by the implications of that single decision—so small yet so impactful. As with all the other rangers I have met, he could never live in a city or work in an office. I envy his fortune at having a job that is not like a job at all.

As we drive, my joy is evident when I see a female nyala, having not seen one since the early days at Moholoholo. The sight of a male nyala excites me even more since I have never seen one. He is impressive with a slate-grey coat and one-twist horns, his lower legs still the colour of caramel from his juvenile years. I look around to the volunteers sitting behind me expecting to see them share in the delight. Instead, flashes of annoyance suggest they do not understand my excitement. I sense something else too—displeasure that I have J.P.'s undivided attention.

On we go, until the beeps from the telemetry tell us that we are getting closer to the lion. We stop in the thicket, peering through the branches. As my eyes adjust and make sense of the tangled web of branches, I see him. Stopping briefly from grooming his golden coat, he looks at us with minimal curiosity. He is the first lion I have seen in the wild. A patterning of scars on his face are tales I so wish I could hear.

Noting this lion's location, we head out to the marshes to check the location of two male cheetahs. We find them lying lazily on top of a mound, overlooking a waterhole, watching zebra, wildebeest and warthog with only the mildest of interest. The cheetahs yawn, one rolling onto his back as he stretches, warming his body in the sun. Through my binoculars, those haunting amber eyes stare back and my mind immediately wanders to Bullet. Leaving the cheetahs and driving towards the plains, we spot a lion mating with two females, which ignites a not-so-ladylike conversation that would make even the toughest men blush. Fertile imagination from four twenty to thirty-something single women in a predominately all-female environment, who have experienced more than their fair share of heartache, is unparalleled. J.P. covers his ears in feigned dismay.

Now in search of another collared lion, we drive off-road, permitted only when tracking predators. The telemetry signals that this lion is only metres away but we cannot see him. Although strictly forbidden in all reserves I have been on so far, we stand on the seats, each looking in a different direction. With fingers placed against our foreheads as if searching for a distant horizon, we act like intrepid explorers, seeking out the wild unknowns. We laugh at our antics but the sudden roar and rush of rustling as the lion darts in front of the vehicle halts our imaginings. I gasp and assess the threat. The lion lies back down under a bush, not bothered anymore by our presence. We probably scared him because we unwittingly got too close. My heart pounds for at least ten minutes more. A game ranger with tourists in his safari jeep asks us for the lion's location. They will have a great sighting but they will not have the excitement we just had.

We stop at a watering hole to admire a large female black rhino and her baby. As our sports-commentator assessment of the situation unfolds, our bets are on the female rhino to charge at the two smaller male rhino wandering a bit too close. To our surprise, it is the baby and not the female who charges at the males, sending them in the opposite direction. We decide that the males knew that they would have no chance against a female protecting her young. Whether that was the case or not did not matter to us. We laugh and as we drive off, our elucidation continues.

Driving for so many hours feels entirely different at Phinda than at Tuli. With seven distinct ecosystems, the changing landscape is a continuous wonder ranging from woodland to grassland, wetland and forest, interspersed with mountain ranges, river courses, marshes and pans. I press J.P. for the names of the most common plants and animals, delighting in learning the ones with the weirdest or funniest of names. The bubbling kassina, a frog whose call sounds like bubbles through water, joins with the calls of the banded rubber frog and the painted reed frog—the quintessential sound of African nocturnal wildlife. There is the Narina trogon—a well-camouflaged green and red bird, the stink-bushwillow flowers browsed by game and the rainbow skink, a lizard often seen on the rocky pathways and walls. There is rat's tail grass, a shrub called dogweed, and the African milkweed plant resembling delicate Chinese paper lanterns. I feel as if knowing the names of such exotic fauna and flora will bring me closer to uncovering the secrets of a world that is so foreign but yet so innately known. My travel companions seem to grow tired of my thirst for this knowledge but J.P. is only happy to oblige. Returning home with only being able to say I saw 'different types of antelope' or 'different types of trees' would be to me a waste of my good fortune at being here in the first place. I shudder at the thought of joining the ranks of lazy tourists.

As we head back to the house, we stop at the Ximhungwe Dam to admire a herd of elephants gathered on its banks. The sound of the bubbling kassina frogs as they engage in their calls adds additional layers of magic and allure. I am so captivated by this scene that I capture it on film, panning occasionally to keep a watchful eye on the elephant grazing not far behind our vehicle. Then we pass whitish clumps hanging from trees containing hundreds of eggs of the grey foam-nest tree frog. We also pass trees whose bark is decidedly yellow in colour. J.P. grants my request to get out of the Landy to touch the fine yellow dust of a fever tree. I decide that this is my favourite tree.

As darkness falls, we find ourselves behind a lone male wildebeest on the narrow, winding dusty road. Amid fits of laughter at this "traffic jam", we call to the wildebeest, asking him kindly to give us passage but our cries go unheeded. Our hopes rise as we approach a fork but the wildebeest does not choose the road less travelled. Where else in the world can you be stuck behind a wildebeest? Eventually, he jumps into the grass and we wish him a good night.

Ngoya ('Savage' in Umbundu) is a collared female leopard. The battery on her collar is running low after two years and is in need of replacing. Having only seen a leopard in captivity and fleeting glimpses of one at Tuli, I am eager to see a wild one up close. The plan for replacing the battery is simple—in theory. Kill a prey animal for bait, locate the leopard, dart when in range, change the battery and leave once the leopard is awake.

Tristan, the research assistant, and Simon, a manager at Phinda, set off in a Land Cruiser to find suitable bait. It is late afternoon now, so they must work quickly before it gets dark. With J.P. at the wheel of a bakkie, he drives us to where Ngoya was last located. We wait. I hear a gunshot ring out in the distance. Returning with a sub-adult male nyala, Tristan asks us if we mind if he puts it in the back of our pickup truck. I do not have any reason to protest. I have witnessed an impala and a gemsbok being dragged behind a car and I have seen a half-eaten wildebeest. I have seen more dead animals in various stages of dismemberment in the past ten weeks than I have in my entire life. The others are the first to see the dead nyala on the ground. They look at each other and almost in unison tell me I should avert my gaze because, as a vegetarian, I must naturally be more sensitive to the sight of dead animals. Ignoring their undue concern, I peer over their shoulders. Half of the nyala's head is missing. This sub-adult male still has his coat of caramel. There is no time for me to indulge in my feelings of sadness.

The nyala now at our feet in the back of the bakkie, we head to where Ngoya was last located. After tying the nyala to a tree out of reach of hyenas, we play the sound of a distressed warthog through speakers. The ear-piercing squeal fills the air. From a distance, I can make out Ngoya's shape. While she approaches this tantalising meal, Tristan and Simon head off with their dart gun.

For two hours, we wait. We laugh that we could well be attacked by lions attracted to the stench of nyala blood congealing on the pick-up truck floor. Tristan and Simon return disappointed. A bush baby sneezed and frightened Ngoya away just moments before they released the dart. Hiding in the dense thicket, a clear shot was impossible. The plan will have to be attempted another day.

The next morning, we drive around the grasslands to note the location of rhino and lions. Among the grasses, we spot a male lion dragging away a freshly killed zebra. To our added delight, one lioness appears to our left, stretching and staring at us with her yellow eyes. The other, on our right, watches us with minimal interest. All eyes are on her as she transitions from her seated position to slowly walking towards our stationary vehicle. From about twenty feet away I look at her without the slightest concern. Fifteen feet. Now ten feet away. Unprotected in an open safari truck and an easy target, wild thoughts are racing through my head. Her demeanour and beauty belie her ferocity, and now I imagine that a mauling by a lion must be a painful death. Having just eaten her share of the zebra, she cannot be hungry, I tell myself. My heart hammers, or maybe it comes to a standstill. The lioness is no more than a few feet away. I glance over at J.P., calm and unaware of what I am imagining could befall us. Fixated on the feline's movements, I hold my breath. We watch as she walks casually past us. We collectively exhale and laugh in combined relief and exhilaration, asking each other just how scared each of us were. Unlike some, I did not mind admitting the truth.

Giddy from the thrill of the lioness encounter, we find a herd of nine black rhino, a rare sight it seems. Noting their location, we leave them behind. We slow as we approach Steve, an enormous and cranky bull elephant. He is flapping his ears to cool himself in the almost unbearable heat. We take advantage of his poor eyesight and watch him for a while, noting his markings and logging his location. Then he spots us. At about a hundred feet, he is a safe distance away. I watch fixated as this grey behemoth comes closer. Forty feet, thirty feet. At twenty feet away, I can see the lines in his trunk a bit too clearly. That familiar sense of unease rises. J.P., nonplussed, starts the engine and reverses. We soon put distance between us. I wonder if J.P. is deliberately trying to scare us.

Five minutes later, we find ourselves in the path of a female elephant. She walks quickly towards us, filling the space between the trees. Everything is happening in slow motion. Why aren't we moving yet? In a whisper layered with alarm and dismay, I tell J.P. that I think we need to go. He is neither looking in her direction nor displaying any hint of concern. Before I can urge him again, he reverses and explains that the elephant was only mildly irritated because she was not trumpeting or shaking her head. Two adrenaline-charged moments in the space of five minutes is suiting me just fine. Our drives are peppered with the thrill of close encounters with dangerous animals that pose no real danger. Underneath it all, I trust J.P. implicitly and without question.

The plan the next day is to dart either a male leopard called Jongozi ('Strong ox' in Zulu) or Ngoya. At 6 a.m., it feels cooler than normal. Rain has not fallen in weeks and there is hope that there will be rain today. For three hours, we drive without a single beep from the telemetry. Tristan decides to change tactic and search for Menzi ('Creator' in Zulu), another male leopard, in the hopes of finding Ngoya or Jongozi close by. Beeps from Menzi's collar give us renewed encouragement and we drive on until the beeps are strong and insistent. Tristan tells us that he must be in the thicket to our left. I look. I look hard, peering through the spaces of the tangled branches and into the darkness of the forest behind. We cannot see him. Using the short-range telemetry, Tristan assures us that Menzi cannot be more than a few feet away. We slowly inch forward. I am dumbfounded how such a large creature can remain invisible to five sets of curious eyes. Suddenly I see him, as if he decided to make himself visible at the flick of a switch. I am speechless as I gaze upon this glorious creature. Tristan grants us ten minutes to enjoy this rare sight. My mind wanders to the sickening pursuits of trophy hunters, poachers, animal traffickers and those who wear leopard skin as religious dress. The only trophy I will bring home will be that of indescribable memories. We reverse and leave him be. Plans for darting are postponed until the following day.

We look to the sky. Rolling black clouds brewing up ahead feel menacing over the grassy plains. The air is heavy and oppressive, and the fading light paints the landscape as if I have never seen it before. We must hurry back before the heavens open up. A clap of thunder makes me jump. Making herself as small as possible, Faye covers her ears in terror. I find this amusing since she has no fear of catching, killing and dissecting rodents for her PhD research, the remnants of which I have seen at breakfast. Driving faster still, I fix my eyes on the horizon, consummately enthralled and captivated by the power and beauty of the storm. Nearing the house, I jump out to open a gate. As the vehicle passes through in the semi-darkness, I make out the shape of a giraffe behind the bushes. I jump back into the green machine, loving this job as gate opener. With just a mile between us and the house, we speed along even faster. We arrive only moments before the torrential rain batters the ground.

Karen, my roommate, and I gleefully dissect the day's events. While getting ready for bed, I notice we have company in the form of various insects. Cupping the dragonfly and the smaller brown praying mantis in my hand, I free them from the confines of our room and into the world outside. I decide that the large green praying mantis can stay. I would like to watch him a while but my lids feel heavy. I fall asleep to the sound of bats in the roof.

Up again at 5.30 a.m., I glance out the front door. The umbrella thorn acacia looks beautiful in the morning light. This is my second favourite tree. An old female nyala is eating grass under the canopy. She is terribly thin, and I wonder if I will see her tomorrow. Once, I tried to approach her in the faint hope that she would allow me to touch her. Before I could get too close, she walked away. I kicked myself for scaring her.

A call from Tristan through the CB radio tells us that he has just killed an impala for either Ngoya or Jongozi's capture later that evening. We drive to meet him, say goodbye to J.P., and join Tristan in his Landy. A little way down the road, Tristan pulls the impala out from the vehicle. I am relieved that the animal is already dead because I do not feel I could face watching an animal being shot—not now, not ever. A hiss of air releases from the impala as Tristan makes a slit in its stomach. The impala now tied to the tree, sounds of a dying warthog blare through speakers.

For six hours, we drive to different locations looking for Ngoya and Jongozi on this 23,000-hectare reserve. With no signal at all from Ngoya, it is as if she has disappeared into thin air. We find leopard tracks belonging to Jongozi along one of the fence lines. It seems he has gone into another property. We cannot call him back this way because Menzi is too close. Leopards are territorial and solitary animals, not liking to be too close to one another. This is not a good location to lay bait either. The road is too near the tourist lodges and too many cars pass in this direction. There is no choice but to postpone.

During my second and final week at Phinda, Rachel and I are the only volunteers. We stand at the doorway of the farmhouse with coffees in hand to ease us into the day ahead, which is still unplanned. Rachel puffs on yet another cigarette while I once again strategically position myself away from the noxious wafts. The sun has barely risen and my gaze is fixed on the lone umbrella thorn acacia, the light bathing it in a way so different than the day before. The old nyala is not in her usual place, in the shade of the verdant canopy. I convince myself that she is safe with her herd rather than having succumbed to nature's end. All is quiet. Peaceful. Although the gentleness of the morning is soothing, I wish to squeeze every last drop out of the few days that remain. I have become a thrill junkie, constantly in pursuit of my next adrenaline fix. I need at least one more hit before I leave.

The sound of the Landy and the smell of diesel rouses me from my thoughtful reverie. Without getting out of the vehicle, Tristan relays three messages—*Join him while he looks for an animal to kill for bait—He understands if we do not wish to—We do not have to witness the kill.* In a split second, my brain evaluates the message imparted, calculating the countless permutations and ramifications of my decision. My id wonders if I will be seen as weak. My ego does not want to be viewed as such. Will I miss out? Will I regret not having this experience? Will I watch? How can I go? I'm tougher than I think. But, wait, we are going now to *kill* an animal.

My adrenaline-junkie brain is already in the Landy. Towards the residential perimeter gate we go, stopping only for a tiny terrapin on the dusty road in front. I jump out and pick up this tiny creature, placing him gently on the palm of my hand. Driving a little further on, I lay him down softly next to a pool of water, relieving him of a long walk to his rightful home. I remonstrate him for putting himself in harm's way and tell him that he is much safer now.

For an hour, we drive through the sand forest and thornveld, slowing at times to peer through the bushes and trees. No nyala. None at all. My junkie brain dozes for a few seconds. The sudden realisation of where I am and what I am doing is stirring a bilious sensation in the pit of my stomach and forming a lump in my throat. My breathing quickens and a wave of cold sweat is making me feel dizzy. I want to stop the trees from rushing past me, to stop us going headlong towards an act I know is tragically necessary. I want to get out. I see myself running through the grasses, through the bushes and back to the sanctuary of the farmhouse, but the trees rushing past me will not be still.

We slow and stop again. Tristan picks up his .308 calibre rifle that was laying on the passenger seat. The sub-adult nyala retreats too far into the thicket, presumably due to the sound of the vehicle. While Tristan is disappointed, I am thrilled. This male gets to live yet another day. We drive on. Another nyala. With rifle cocked, the shot is impossible. We leave him be. While Rachel and Tristan discuss their disappointment, I busy myself with my bootlaces to conceal my burgeoning relief. My jaws ache from clenching my teeth in an effort to forbid my face to reveal my true feelings but I know the inevitable is near.

We find a sub-adult male standing with a few females. My eyes dart back and forth from the slate-grey nyala to the mahogany of the rifle. With an unobstructed view, Tristan prepares. I do not want to watch this. I cannot. I will not. My feet are resting against the metal bar separating the first banquette and the driver's seat. Placing my head on my bent knees that are now pressed tightly against my chest, I scrunch my eyes until it hurts and put my fingers in my ears. Everything is silent except for the hammering of my heart, my laboured breathing and the throbbing in my ears. The gunshot makes me jump. Uncrumpling myself, I look to my left. The nyala is dead, lying on the ground, the females still close to him. Time stands still. No one moves. The females freeze, confused about why their male counterpart is now on the ground when only seconds before he was munching on the grass. Nothing indicates the presence of a predator.

As we drive closer, the hum of the vehicles scares the females. They run away, barking their alarm calls to alert others of the apparent but unseen danger. Their cries are heart-rending. I stand up in the Landy and look down at the nyala, his body twitching and legs kicking. His diaphragm is moving up and down as if breathing. Keeping my composure to conceal my horror that the nyala might still be alive in the throes of an excruciatingly painful death, I ask Tristan in a voice that does not sound like mine if the nyala is still alive. Tristan assures me that the nyala is dead and the twitching I am witnessing are the reflexes. I search his face and I see that he has remembered that although he has become accustomed to killing animals for bait, I am not yet inured to these experiences. That realisation softens his face a little. To convince me further, he bends down to touch the black orbs staring into the distance. He looks up at me, my face revealing that I am desperate to believe him. The still-twitching nyala does not blink.

With no time to process what my eyes have just seen, I help load the nyala into the back of the Land Cruiser. I pick up his back legs and feel the warmth of his body, my brain still trying to convince me that he must be alive. Only the gurgling of blood as it oozes out of the gash in his head convinces me he is not.

We drive to Ngoya's last known location, through the Avatar-esque sand forest approximately thirty kilometres from the farmhouse. She appears on the road in front of us, attracted to the sound of a dying warthog playing through speakers. We follow her but she slinks back into the thicket. Now 6 p.m., it is getting dark. With the spotlight on her, we can see that she is facing us, but Tristan cannot take a clear shot. He cuts off one of the nyala's ears and throws it onto the road to entice Ngoya out again. We wait, silently. Without the engine hum, chatter or crackled voices from the

CB radio, I can hear the forest. Really hear it. Uninterrupted. I hear every bird, the grasshoppers and the cacophony of sounds that surround us. Darkness has fallen thick and fast and I shine the red spotlight in an effort to avoid blinding her. Ngoya moves out of sight. We inch forward and then back. We see her again. An hour passes and Ngoya will not come out to take the ear lying on the road.

To entice her even further, Tristan cuts off one of the nyala's legs and throws it on the ground. We wait. Another hour passes. Tristan decides that he must tie the whole nyala to the tree. Leaving the safety of the Land Cruiser, he is putting himself in danger with a leopard so close by. Tristan returns and we wait. After ten minutes, we shine the spotlight, and yet again she darts into the thicket. We wait. We find her again, the night spotlight bathing her in a blood-red hue. We wait until she stands up to dart her in the rump. Ngoya stands and I hold my breath. Tristan fires but Ngoya dashes to the left. He curses since he is quite sure he missed, not hearing the sound a dart makes upon contact with an animal. Leaving a tranquillized leopard is very dangerous as she would be susceptible to lions. If she is not darted and he tracks her on foot, she could attack him. Now the circle of trust, as he calls it, is broken. Tristan is visibly annoyed because he has worked for months to build her trust so that he can approach her without her disappearing. Regaining that trust will be difficult. He admits that he should not have taken the shot. After a few minutes, we see her walking through the bushes. The dart missed. Defeated, we head back to the farmhouse.

The following day at 5 p.m., Rachel and I join Tristan in the green machine. I am relieved to be doing something other than torturing myself with thoughts of my imminent departure. A putrid smell from the vehicle prompts me to look in the back. It is a leg from the nyala. We will need it now to entice Ngoya yet again. The beeps on the telemetry indicate that Zumba, her fourteen-month-old cub is close by. We spot Zumba in the thicket, but we do not need to dart him. Ngoya is calling him, but Zumba does not answer back, too interested in the smell emanating from the vehicle. His mother calls again, but he does not respond. We hope that she will come out to fetch him.

We have no option but to wait here, deep within the sand forest, the darkness casting scary shadows from the overhanging trees with twisted branches. It is going to be a long wait. I slide myself down the seat until my head rests on the metal bar behind. I look up into the sky through the leaves dancing overhead. A storm is brewing. All is dark except for the continuous flashes of lightning like a fluorescent bulb flickering before its light is steady. I close my eyes and bid myself to listen. It is so quiet that I can hear Rachel and Tristan breathing and the gurgling of our stomachs. Still we wait. My right leg is going numb and my eyelids are heavy. I am hesitant to move because we have to be as still as possible to not scare Ngoya away. Every fifteen minutes, we shine the light to see if Ngoya has come any closer. Still we wait.

A call on the CB from J.P. parked a little distance away, tells us he has picked up Ngoya's signal in a different location. After much searching, we find them both. Zumba is closer to us but Ngoya is too far away. We can still see her eyes shining back at us from the light of the spotlight. The problem now is that there is a large felled tree blocking our path. We need both of them to come forward. Zumba comes closer and I can see him clearly now. I feel myself taking a sharp intake of breath as I gaze upon his face, angular and long. Swathed in the blood-red light from the spotlight filter, I film him until I run out of memory, knowing I will never be this close to a leopard ever again. Then Tristan urges us to be very still since Zumba is about to charge at us. Zumba hisses. He is ten feet away. Even though he is only fourteen months old, he could do serious damage to any one of us. Trying to calm my heavy breathing as it punctuates the heavy silence, Tristan shouts at Zumba to back off and he does. We reverse and head off in search of another way to get closer to Ngoya but bushes and trees block the route.

Then we see Ngoya behind the car about fifty feet away. Tristan cocks his dart gun and fires. He misses. The distance calculator is broken and he overestimated. She slinks off into the thicket. Visibly annoyed, Tristan drives to where the dart would have landed to double check that he missed. While I keep the spotlight on Zumba, Tristan gets out of the vehicle to find the dart. Zumba hears the rustling and starts walking towards Tristan. I call out to tell him that Zumba is walking in his direction. A few seconds later, Tristan is safely back in the vehicle. At 10 p.m. we head back, admitting defeat yet again.

When J.P. picks us up the next morning, I tell him that since it is my last day, I am desperate for another hit of adrenaline, enough to carry me into the unknown in the weeks that lay ahead and to numb me from the rising dread of leaving a life I have come to adore. From his smile, I know I will not be disappointed. Out the gate we go and into the bush, slowing only when we see a bull elephant walking in our direction on the narrow road. The elephant takes up the entire width of the road, his enormous ears almost touching the leaves of the trees. We cannot pass him. We watch him approach, blocking more of the sunlight as he moves closer.

I wonder how long it will be before J.P. reverses. That familiar feeling is creeping through my veins. J.P. reverses a little and then into a clearing in the trees on the right. The elephant is still walking towards us, towering over the trees. Rachel and J.P. assure me that the elephant will simply walk past us, but I do not believe them. While an elephant's eyesight is poor, their sense of smell is not. The elephant comes closer still. The scene seems to play out in slow motion. The elephant is approaching, still perpendicular to the car. He does not keep walking, instead he turns into the clearing and is only feet away. My world goes grey and the low rumbling is terrifying. Finally, J.P. heeds my pleas and reverses at breakneck speed with the elephant charging at us. We quickly put distance between us and I can finally breathe. J.P. laughs and reminds me that he is simply giving me what I asked for.

As we wind around the dusty trails, J.P. asks me if I

am scared of roller coasters. I nod fervently. That was the wrong answer. With the accelerator pressed to the floor, we speed down a very steep hill and up the next one. Coming to a stop, I am breathless, exhilarated and nauseous, unsure if I want to thank or remonstrate J.P. who is relishing in providing us with unforgettable thrills.

Our giddiness is contagious and we laugh at the simplest of things. To add to our antics even more, Rachel suggests filming me as though I am running very fast through the grass. I am in the mood for tomfoolery today, desperate to cling on to the joy and freedom I feel every day at Phinda. Standing up, I steady myself by leaning one of my thighs against the metal bar. "Ready, steady go!" I move my arms in a running motion. J.P. presses the accelerator to the floor and we speed along. The radio DJ type commentary begins, "…and Sonia is first in line and putting great distance between her and the other runners. She is in fine form. Look at her go!" For a few more minutes the commentary continues.

The need to press my thighs even more against the bar becomes greater to avoid falling over from the speed and from laughter I can barely contain. The wind is blowing against my face and I am up high, speeding along windy rust-coloured tracks between yellow grasses almost as tall as I am on each side. I wish to go faster and faster still. I feel as if I am truly running, running deeper into the arms of exhilaration found in the wide-open spaces of South Africa. The euphoria envelops me, deeply and profoundly. Then finally J.P. takes his foot off the accelerator and we start to slow. "Sonia, slow down, slow down!" J.P. continues with his commentary. "To the finish line!" Rachel adds. I throw my hands up in the air and beam at the invisible crowd who are cheering and clapping at my victory. Sitting back down, I throw my head back and laugh even more. My cheeks and stomach hurt from so much silliness.

We arrive back by late afternoon and I flop down onto the couch in the small living room. Soon, Faye and the others students join us and I recount my thrill of running through the grass, with Rachel and J.P. adding in their commentary for added effect. Another bout of laughter ensues. As I look around at my Phinda companions, I am so immensely and blissfully happy. I will miss each and every one of them.

Late into the night, I pack for the last time, a moment that I have been afraid of for weeks. Each time these thoughts ran through my mind, I immediately sent them scurrying and relegated them to a box labelled "later". Over the past month, I refused to let all feelings of dread taint any moment here in Africa. Now, I must face the consequences of all that suppressed dread as it scrambles furiously out of the "later" box that is no longer strong enough to keep it contained.

A call from my mother regarding some trivial matter that needs my *urgent attention* once I am back home prickles my skin with blistering annoyance. Throwing the phone on my bed, I stomp into the kitchen, fling open the door and run outside. Out in the cool night air, I bend over, clutching my stomach. Unable to breathe, I have an overwhelming need to be sick. My legs feel wobbly and I lower my head to ease the dizziness and sudden light-headedness. All I can do is wait while the forces within me battle it out.

Eventually I go back inside and throw the last remaining items into my backpack, not caring if they are placed neatly or uniformly, or in the compartments they have been meticulously assigned to since my arrival. I am too tired to care and too tired to force the zip that refuses to close. I collapse into bed and fall asleep. There are no bats in the roof this night.

In the morning, there are warm hugs goodbye, pictures taken and promises to keep in touch. My genuine affection for my Phinda companions and our exchanges keep my mind off the journey that lays in front of me. I sling my backpack into the back seat of the transfer van, wrinkling my nose at the smell of the leather upholstery. As we set off, I look out the back window. My Phinda friends are waving me goodbye, still gathered by the kitchen door. I wave back, catching one last glimpse of the umbrella thorn acacia and the old, sick nyala under the shade of the canopy.

My parents push through the crowds of people in the arrivals hall in Dublin airport, running at me, arms outstretched for at least ten paces before wrapping themselves around me. For the first few days, I busy myself with connecting and meeting with a few old friends. The repetition of my adventures in Africa helps to sustain the euphoria and joy I am desperate to cling to. I go for a much-needed haircut and upload all my photographs onto my computer. It feels good to be back in my double bed, to have neatly folded clothes smelling of fabric conditioner.

For the first time in three months, I look in a full-length mirror, unable to recognise the girl staring back. My skin is a shade somewhere between bronze and deep mahogany. The jeans that were a little too tight before I left, now fall down without a belt. There is something else too, a confidence and poise that I have never seen before, standing straighter, taller, with my head held high.

Soon the first flush of excitement of being back home—a place where I do not have to check my shoes for insects, nor my bed for spiders—wears off, and the overwhelming decision of where I will go to next dawns upon me. Every morning, just before I wake, there are a few moments where I believe I am still in Africa and my body is bathed in a glow of this comfort. Then with the realisation that I am not, the cold river of anxiety rushes in to take its place.

The first few months in Dublin pass by in a blur of unproductivity and uncertainty. Job applications in conservation-related fields in Vancouver go unanswered. I have always wanted to move there, a city where the Pacific Ocean and coastal mountains meet, a city brimming with environmental consciousness. The monumental task of moving city again leaves me overwhelmed. The burden of facing this task alone makes me want to retreat inside myself, to a place I have spent the last three months running from. I do not get up before noon.

City life is insufferable, a beastly collision of greyness, and incessant noise that leaves me inert, numb and listless. Trips to the shopping centre are unbearable and an assault on the senses. The music blaring from each shop makes me want to cover my ears. People bump into me, unapologetically. There are no plants, trees or anything resembling the natural environment. The fluorescent lights make my head pound. It is claustrophobic. I feel hemmed in, suffocated by the artificiality. The sickly sweet smell of doughnuts mixed with competing aromas from the food court curdles my rising nausea. Too many people, like an overcrowded termite mound, scuttle in their pointless pursuit of things they do not really need. I walk around in a zombie-like stupor wanting to run, run as fast as I can away from this oppressive, stifling, concrete box filled with stuff. Meaningless, useless stuff.

Searching for ways to make this transition between chapters in my life a little more palatable, I call Kirsten and Daniel. Our conversations are joyous and animated, providing me with some reprieve from the path I am on, one of uncertainty.

At 3 p.m. each day, I settle into the white leather couch, turn on the TV to a wildlife channel and wait in anticipation. This time the game ranger is animated. There is a large bull elephant ahead and silence now is paramount. With everyone quiet, the game ranger isolates the sounds that make up the cacophony, imitating each one as he identifies them. The Cape turtle dove, the crested francolin, the African fish eagle, and the trumpet of elephants in the distance. In hushed whispers, he relays facts about a particular elephant. The tension is high since poachers have been spotted in the area. I listen intently, allowing the sights and sounds of the African bush to penetrate my being. So comforting, nurturing. Immersed, engrossed and wholly present with the people on the bush walk, I watch transfixed, barely moving, drinking in the scene, knowing the scenery and sounds with such intimacy, even naming the birds in my head. All too soon, the TV programme ends. I am still, unable to move. The white leather sofa is cold against my skin. The soul-crushing emptiness returns.

One evening, as I lie in bed looking out of the floor-to-ceiling window in my parents' sixth-floor apartment, I watch the twinkling city lights and ponder the invitation in my hand. My initial reaction was to throw it in the bin, wanting to be rid of this rectangular card with fancy fonts that caused a rush of unwanted memories to flood my mind. Then I considered that the outcome might not be so bad. I stare at the card awhile, glancing occasionally out of my window as the thoughts as to whether or not I should attend whirl around my brain. Finally, I decide that I will go, but that I will leave after an hour if it is not to my liking. This "escape" clause lowers my anxiety. The following day, I go shopping for the perfect outfit befitting of my twenty-year secondary school reunion in just over a week.

The taxi pulls up in front of the five-star hotel. As I open the car door, I take a deep breath and tuck my black clutch bag with a gold handle under my arm. The pebbles along the path to the front door are difficult to walk on with the four-inch heels of my silver shoes. A sign in the lobby denotes that the reunion is on the lower floor. I stop at the top of the stairs. Some of my colleagues are standing at a podium at the bottom greeting arriving guests. As I descend, they look up. They stare at me. One has his mouth open. I can tell they are scanning their memory bank as to whom I might be. As I glide down the stairs, my sleeveless, knee-length, gold-laced silver dress sparkles under the pot lights. Reaching the bottom, I am greeted with tight hugs and warm kisses. I need not have worried about my former classmates' reaction.

Glancing over their shoulders and into the crowded room, I immediately spot the boy who bullied me, the one who reminded me on a nearly weekly basis that I had a beak on my face. I turn to the girl standing beside me and tell her whom I have just seen and ask if she knew that he had bullied me for years. "Go tell him off and tell him I told you to!" she says. I laugh, but my initial reaction is to disregard her advice. I spent years and years rehearsing what I would say to him if I ever bumped into him again, but I never got my chance. I did not care now either. It was two decades ago. I enter the room; it is heaving with people. Many hours pass engrossed in lively conversation, swapping tales of students we fancied, teachers we disliked and where life had led us. Reconnecting with my classmates feels like sunshine on a cool day, and all my feelings of apprehension float away. My cheeks hurt from smiling and my voice is now hoarse.

By 3 a.m., my feet ache and I am desperate to free them from my shoes that are far more stylish than they are comfortable. Dizzy from tiredness, I head for the exit and wave goodbye to a group standing by the door. "I didn't tell you how beautiful you look tonight." I stop dead in my tracks and look around, knowing immediately to whom that voice belongs. Without thinking I respond, "That's interesting you say that because you told me I was ugly every day." There is silence for a moment and then a rush of denial of how that was not possible since his father bullied him. I smile sweetly, unperturbed. I tell him matter-of-factly that I know this for sure. Just the previous week I had rummaged in the back of my parents' wardrobe and hauled out a pink plastic box containing the diaries I wrote over a ten-year period. I had re-read them late into the night, partly in an attempt to find closure to a past that still troubled me and partly to ascertain if my memories were accurate. I came across an entry that said, "He punched me in the stomach today, but I didn't tell anyone." The boys standing with him slap him on the back and tell him to say sorry. They even say sorry on his behalf. I laugh at these men who are still just boys in lots of ways. I stand there, smiling confidently, unflustered by his denial. Then comes twenty minutes of apologies, which I accept graciously. I smile outwardly, but most of all, I smile inside. Not because I had finally received the apology I had waited for, but because I knew that those experiences no longer had a hold over me.

The following day, still sleepy from getting home in the early hours of the morning, I spot an email from Laura. I had not been in touch with her for some weeks because my next steps were yet undecided. I felt twinges of pain each time she told me how Bandit was. She interpreted these long periods of silence from me as my wish never to return for Bandit at all. In her email, she threatened to bring Bandit to the nearest animal shelter if I did not pick her up in the next few weeks. I had not expected this response at all. Alice had handed Bandit over to Laura a month earlier, having grown tired of looking after her. Now Bandit was an inconvenience for Laura too. I had left both women with enough cat food to last nearly a year and money had been left on account at my local vet should they need further provisions. They were not out-of-pocket for anything. All I asked was that they showered Bandit with love.

This email from Laura forces me to make a decision. I sign up for a three-month French language course in Quebec City, making a mental note not to adopt the wince-inducing accent. A month later, I fly to Toronto. Unceremoniously, I put Bandit into her pet carrier, eager to relieve Laura of her apparent burden. Later that night, Bandit lays on my pillow and I kneel on the floor beside her with my elbows on the bed. Bandit's demeanour signals that she is not pleased and I do not see any sign that she remembers me. I tell her that I am so desperately sorry for leaving her and that I will never leave her again. Not ever. I implore her to forgive me. In that moment, she blinks and stretches, inviting me to rub my head on hers—head butts, we call it. Bandit is mine again. The following day, Bandit and I fly to Quebec City.

Comforted by the warm summer days, new friends, a part-time job in an open-air farmer's market and pleased by my daily linguistic achievements, I extend my stay indefinitely. A very handsome man gives me another reason to stay. We met at a Friday night dinner, hosted every week by the head of the Jewish community. Over the years, I had seen this man many times in my dreams, never his face, but I was familiar with his energy. The first time I met him, it was as if I knew him already. The Jewish community was small, mainly made up of students staying only for a few months or a few years. Everyone knew everyone else. Most were from France. It was obvious by the way the other girls at the dinner table looked at him that they all fancied him. Their lingering glances, the way they played with their hair, the flirtatious comments and coy smiles. He wanted to keep our relationship hidden, not ready to share the news. The weeks went by. Week after week, I sat at the same table and pretended I was only a casual acquaintance. Eventually, I gave him an ultimatum: tell everyone, or the relationship was over. The man of my dreams ended our relationship, the same week he discovered that I was more than ten years his senior. Not looking my age, people always assume, even now, that I am ten years younger than I am. His exit coincided with the departure of the friends I had made at the language school, who were now returning home in other countries. Worn out by the emptiness and the grip of a frigid winter, I wait until the following summer to move to Ottawa.

Moving apartment three times within the space of six weeks, I finally find a quiet, modern place with a girl and her three cats. The apartment is a peaceful haven for job hunting—at first. A few days after I move in, I find myself subjected to the unrelenting percussion of a jackhammer tearing up the road only feet from my bedroom window. From morning until night, for weeks on end, the deafening drilling continues with no reprieve. With no end in sight and unable to cope with the maddening, incessant racket, I move into an apartment of my own.

Shortly before I start a new four-month contract, I spend three long, gruelling days unpacking the boxes I had left in a storage unit. At first, I am elated to be working at a division of a federal government department in the capital city. This new position tackling issues related to endangered wildlife will end several months of unemployment. Beginning to believe my luck is finally starting to change, I tell myself that such a fortuitous opportunity is why all the other job applications went unanswered. My optimism was short-lived. Right from the first day, I sensed that this contract would not be without incident. My boss would glare at me over the cubicle wall and bark her orders. Although she lavished praise on the only male member of the team, she subjected the rest of us to her harsh criticism. My work was never good enough in her eyes, even though others in related divisions praised me for my efficiency and tenacity to get up to speed in an area I knew very little about. In meetings, she did not allow any of her team to speak.

On one particular Friday afternoon, although it was not part of my job description, she instructed me to find a solution to a problem that no one else, not even subject matter experts, had been able to solve. I had until Monday. The blood drained from my face, but there was no use in protesting; being a contractor and not a permanent employee made me vulnerable to termination. Protected by senior management, she had free reign to inflict her misery until I completed the contract.

Despite this experience, I still refuse to let go of this path, this continued pursuit of a position based on pay and other people's perceptions of success. I hold onto it with a vice-like grip and eyes tightly shut. The result is a two-month contract. Although this new job is well paid and also related to endangered wildlife, I am working almost entirely alone in an airless, windowless library on a cold, grey university campus in the depths of winter.

In April, I leave Bandit with a neighbour and fly to Venice for a week to meet up with my parents. Rejuvenated by the warmth of the Venetian sun, I fly back to Ottawa for another four-month contract. Although I am thrilled to see Bandit, coming home to a harsh minus 22°C and a silent flat makes me feel as vacuous as my empty fridge. I spend the four days before I start work completely alone; there is no one to meet up with or chat to on the phone.

From the floor to ceiling windows of my twelfth-floor apartment, I overlook the ByWard Market. Snow swirls through the street below, driven by gusts of icy wind before landing delicately on muddy slush and frozen puddles. The barren greyness of the city is enshrouded by a sheet of sparkling brilliant-white—pristine but temporary. I close my eyes. After twelve months, I can identify the sounds that surround me with unerring accuracy. There is no peace here. Every moment is filled with the constant whirring of industrial generators from the buildings below. Incessant clanging, drilling and hammering reverberate from the construction of new apartments just a stone's throw away. Snowploughs ring out their high-pitched chirp. Somewhere close by, a multi-frequency backup alarm and a locator tone on a traffic light beep yet again. The maddening din echoes within me, resounding against my being as thunderously as the jackhammer just beyond. I flash open my eyes as though startled. Remaining perfectly still, I listen closely. There, among the tempestuous dissonance, barely audible whispers weave their way through the torrent of discord. At that precise moment, I know I will leave Canada once my contract is over.

At this four-month contract, my office is a high-walled cubicle where conversation is discouraged. Although my manager's office is only at the end of the corridor, she does not speak to me for days, preferring instructions by email. A co-worker forcing mucus down his throat in retch-inducing snorts is the only sound that breaks the oppressive silence.

Almost three years to the day after returning to Canada, I board a flight to Dublin. Upon arrival, and despite travelling in cargo, Bandit is far less worse for wear than I after our fifteen-hour journey. All of my belongings are in a shipping container on their way to London. A few months later, I accept a six-month contract in central government and move from Dublin to London with Bandit.

On the morning of my first day at work, I step out of the train carriage at Westminster station and onto the platform, pushed forward by a wave of grey-faced, suit-wearing clones frantically weaving their way through the narrow passageways. Desperate to get to the escalators in the hallway just beyond, I am met with a sea of people arriving at the same time from other directions. With nowhere to turn, I am swallowed up by the flood of commuters converging towards and onto the escalator. The realisation I am back in a cold grey city, ostensibly alone, is too much for me to bear. I vomit onto the pavement only yards from my place of work.

Unexpectedly, this maternity leave contract leads to a better position writing speeches on energy policy for a junior minister. While I am complimented by the minister's office on my aptitude for turning dry policy statements into emotive speeches, my manager is displeased that I am headstrong and do not share the submissive demeanour of his other female subordinates. Senior management and the Permanent Secretary praise my courage for publishing an article about my struggle with anxiety, the publication of which forces change within a department that refused to tackle this subject in any meaningful way and compels countless staff members to seek help. While I found and co-chair the department's first wellbeing and mental health group, I become a threat to the delicate balance of civil servant culture where it is common to appear busy but produce nothing of value. My openness and desire to help others only highlights the inefficiencies and ineffectiveness of those paid to tackle this difficult subject.

Seated in a large, airless, open-plan office among endless rows of people robotically typing on laptops, I close my eyes. The incessant clacking of hundreds of pairs of hands on keyboards feels like fingernails down a chalkboard. The clatter grows louder and increases in intensity, matching my breathing that has now turned shallow and rapid. I want to run. I want to run fast and far from the maddening sound of pretend productivity. With my eyes still closed, I have no choice but to quietly wrangle these feelings inside myself until they subside. I focus on breathing, but these feelings continue to push their way to the surface of my mind. In the whirr of competing emotions to flee or fight, there is something else—a whisper. I strain to listen. It whispers again.

My acrimonious exit coincides with Bandit's passing at the age of twenty and the passing of my next-door neighbour's cat, TomTom, who dies suddenly a week later from a broken heart at losing his best friend. Bandit had spent nearly every day for the past year with my next-door neighbour and his cat while I was at work, comforting me that she was not alone during the day. My flat now is empty, soulless, void of her pitter-patter and her gentle paw on my face to wake me from a nightmare. Without Bandit, I am utterly lost. My life force cut off.

In those days of darkness, without friends, a job or my dearest companion, I spiral into a black abyss. Support from extended family does not come, not now and not since my arrival two years ago. London does not lend itself to popping in for no particular reason, or picking up the phone, or last-minute invitations. Life here is all-consuming, frantic and exhausting, with each family unit keeping to themselves. My life is so different, not easily measured by where I work, to whom I am married or how many children I have. For some, that is uncomfortable and they cannot relate.

Slumped in front of the TV, mindlessly flicking through the channels with only my thoughts for company, I think of Big Boy, how I fell to the ground and wept for days, and how I cried against my life—the life that was and the life that would subsequently unfold in a way I did not want. My life so far felt as though trapped in a pinball machine, circumstances forcing me in directions I did not want to go. I sometimes timed the strike of propulsion, not knowing where the impact would lead, but invariably I found myself, yet again, in an unfavourable position.

During those days despair, the chinks in the armour that Big Boy's roars created grew bigger, letting in light where none had lived before. His roars had made cracks in the walls I built to defend myself against situations that often did not need defending. Not only were there space and light, but there were more whispers. I started not only to listen, but also to hear the message I had been ignoring all along; a message that Big Boy wanted me to hear. *I could no longer hold onto that which refused to be held.*

Determined to claw my way back—back to that peace and joy I had felt in so much abundance in Africa—I fly to Dublin for a month. Instead of being slumped on the couch, I train four times a week for a five-kilometre run. Running in the adjacent park, passing ducks, ponds, dogs, oak trees, grass, hills and streams fills my mind with what is possible and empties my soul of what is not. Each week I run faster and farther.

During this month, an email about joining a franchise pops into my inbox quite unexpectedly. While I try to dismiss my capabilities at running my own business, almost rejecting the idea entirely, again the whispers float gently in my mind. Heeding these whispers, a few months later, I join a dog-walking franchise. Now a business owner with semi-autonomy, I am excited about my future, a path aligned with my values now more than ever before. Unconditional love from the pets in my care nurture my soul and my clients marvel at my gift with animals. Although my business is successful, I find myself spending more time trying to stay ahead of the stiff competition.

Eager to drive more traffic to my site, I accidentally stumble upon a free seminar on internet marketing. I stare at the entry in my diary, scheduled for 6 p.m. that evening, requiring me to brave the cold, wet, wintery February weather and attend a location right next to where I last worked. I think of all sorts of reasons why I do not want to go, but again the whispers come unannounced. I listen. I go. Those two hours in a hotel conference room open up a world I never knew existed, a world of search engine optimisation, Google rankings, and internet marketing, but most of all, a world of financial freedom with total autonomy. I sign up for a three-day online marketing course with the Internet Business School. A few weeks later, I pass the test. Shortly thereafter, after much consideration, I leave the franchise.

The walls of my apartment are cream. In the light of day, they are a shade somewhere between vanilla and buttermilk. Leaning back in my office chair, my legs tucked under a white corner desk, my eyes are drawn to the purple and pink butterflies affixed to the sloping ceiling just above my head. To my left is a Blue Cross calendar with this month's star pet, once abandoned, now in their forever home. Next to that is my vision board; one half is a whiteboard and the other cork. The whiteboard portion displays affirmation statements I have copied from Michelle Buchanan's *The Numerology Guidebook*, statements I read each morning. The cork displays pictures of Nala and other pictures of cats. The phrase "I believe in myself" cut out from a magazine sits next to a cartoon character of a girl surrounded by dogs and cats. Close by is my most prized possession—a canvas print of TomTom sitting behind Bandit, a picture I took only weeks before they passed.

Naiveté led me to believe that going to Africa would fix my problems. I ended up in unwanted situations because I was afraid to listen to my heart, afraid of change and afraid of hearing what I did not want to hear. I do not believe that "what does not kill you makes you stronger". I believe that what does not kill you forces a re-evaluation of your path, however weakened you might be.

The road ahead now is unmapped, but my way forward is clear—at least clear enough to make it to the next junction. With no one to answer to but myself, I can be creative and daring, and implement ideas to my exacting standards rather than wait for permission from those who prefer the status quo. Building numerous income streams through affiliate marketing, book writing and, most exciting of all, building a business to help other small local businesses with their internet marketing is a path I never could have imagined.

Life does not always work out the way we would wish. It is not round, smooth and perfect, rather jagged, with difficult twists and turns to navigate, sometimes blindly. Big Boy gave me a gift, one that is priceless and immeasurable, a gift that words can never describe. He gave me the gift of freedom to stand in my truth—freedom and truth that now help me to navigate those twists and turns, no matter how challenging they may be. Big Boy's whispers gently guided me towards an alignment with who I really am, freeing me from the burden of allowing the opinion of others to drive my emotions, my decisions and the opinion I have of myself.

Each one of us has a lion's roar within ourselves. Finding our roar takes years, sometimes decades. To be free, all we have to do is listen.

Big Boy is now in spirit. Wherever he may be, he will always and forever be in my heart.